Supporting Young Children of Immigrants and Refugees

This text offers a comprehensive portfolio of approaches to support young children with refugee backgrounds. It covers trauma-informed pedagogies, transitioning to school, authentic inclusion, play, social and emotional learning, and intergenerational trauma.

In early childhood centres around the world, teachers and directors can be uncertain of how to meet the needs of newly arrived children. Based on empirical research in five countries, this book offers insights from early childhood educators who are working hard to support families and young children with refugee and asylum-seeker experiences. It illustrates the link between theory and practice and the importance of developing culturally sensitive classroom strategies to effectively support the emotional and cognitive needs of multilingual, multicultural students whose common experiences may only include displacement, trauma, and loss. Rather than offering a measure for 'success,' this book shares the knowledge and experience of practitioners who understand the work and the very particular circumstances of these children's lives. The authors bring these perspectives together in order to inspire other professionals who face this challenging work, encouraging the reader to reflect, to consider how relevant some of the ideas may be in their own contexts, and to contemplate the principles which allow their professional actions to make a difference.

This book is an essential resource for early childhood educators and leaders who want to 'open the door' to genuinely inclusive, empathetic, and supportive practice. It will be of great interest to researchers and postgraduate students in the fields of early childhood and primary education.

Maura Sellars has 30 years' experience as a classroom teacher, followed by over 20 years as a university lecturer. She works within the fields of pedagogy, leadership, cognition, mathematics, and inclusion. She has published widely on numeracy across the curriculum, inclusive school culture, teacher practices, and educating refugee students.

Scott Imig is Associate Professor in the School of Education at the University of Newcastle (AUS). His current research focuses on creating welcoming, safe, and engaging classroom environments for all students. Prior to university life, Scott was a primary teacher and a middle school science teacher in the United States.

Doug Imig is a staff member at Early Childhood Action Strategy, a collective impact organisation in Hawai'i (USA) focused on the health, well-being, and school readiness of young children. Previously, he taught political science and public policy at the University of Memphis.

'While reading, each chapter sparked a flame in my heart, stronger and stronger. As an Early Childhood Teacher, educating refugee children, I feel it's our responsibility to advocate for the rights of all Australian children and advocate for the Early Childhood Profession. The first five years of a child's life is so instrumental to development. Your book is not only highlighting this, but it's advocating for the important role Early Childhood Educators play and how there is a need for policy makers to make changes to better reflect critical needs to support our educators, children, families and communities.'

Clair Robinson, *University of Newcastle, Australia*

'*Supporting Young Children of Immigrants and Refugees*, a scholarly work by multiple authors is a serious and important work about working with children in families with refugee experiences, now resettled into five different, English-speaking countries. The book focuses on the difficulties the children and their families encounter as they are settled in countries very different from their countries of origin. The chapter on 'Trauma' is both comprehensive and compelling as it includes both the initial and lasting effects of the trauma suffered by refugee children. The chapter on children's play also stands out because of the understanding and emphasis on the importance of children's play and the sensitive writing about play. This is an important contribution to knowledge, a useful work for caregivers and other staff at refugee camps and a readable, informative work for policy makers and the general public.'

Joseph M. Hawes, *Professor of History Emeritus, University of Memphis, USA*

Supporting Young Children of Immigrants and Refugees

The Promise and Practices of Early Care and Learning

Maura Sellars, Scott Imig, and Doug Imig

Routledge
Taylor & Francis Group

LONDON AND NEW YORK

Designed cover image: © Getty Images

First published 2024
by Routledge
4 Park Square, Milton Park, Abingdon, Oxon OX14 4RN

and by Routledge
605 Third Avenue, New York, NY 10158

Routledge is an imprint of the Taylor & Francis Group, an informa business

© 2024 Maura Sellars, Scott Imig and Doug Imig

British Library Cataloguing-in-Publication Data
A catalogue record for this book is available from the British Library

ISBN: 9781032518565 (hbk)
ISBN: 9781032518558 (pbk)
ISBN: 9781003404231 (ebk)

DOI: 10.4324/9781003404231

Typeset in Galliard
by KnowledgeWorks Global Ltd.

Contents

Acknowledgements

We would like to sincerely thank our participants who shared their insights, experiences, and passion with us. In the midst of the global diaspora that has forced so many families from their homes and unleashed trauma on the youngest and most vulnerable, these wonderful educators have created places of welcoming and belonging. They give us hope for the future.

We would also like to thank Dr Tra Do for her assistance and support with this work. Her insightful analyses added much to this manuscript.

Introduction

The world refugee crisis is growing rapidly. It is challenging both the limits of the services that welcoming countries can provide for their newcomers and also the mindsets and perspectives of the professionals who work in supportive organisations. This book brings together some of the narratives from educators and carers in early childhood settings who are working hard to meet the challenges of collaborating with and supporting families and young children with refugee and asylum-seeker experiences. These narratives were collected from a very diverse cohort of teachers, carers, and policymakers in five English-speaking countries – Australia, New Zealand, Northern Ireland, England, and the United States – all of whom have been engaged in providing the best opportunities they can manage in their own unique contexts. Their work has demanded that they are creative, innovative, and knowledgeable about the diverse cultural, social, and religious backgrounds of the babies, toddlers, and young children in their care, their families, and their communities.

Their responsibilities call for them to be exceptionally flexible, empathetic, and sensitive in ways that are exclusive to foundational care and education of the very young. In doing this, they participate in the healing processes that are necessary for those in their care, and they also have the task of recognising and accepting the ways in which the very young express their distress. They understand the impact of traumatic events and the effects of intergenerational trauma, some of which remains unacknowledged in the contexts of babies and toddlers whose early language does not facilitate direct communication of their stress. The intention of this work is not to measure the successes of the participants' strategies or to provide exemplary examples that are failproof in any context. Rather, the purpose is to share the experiences of practitioners who understand the situations these young children and their families are placed in, in order to inspire others who may struggle with similar concerns and challenges in their professional lives. The purpose is also to inform readers of the theory that may allow a more educated, nuanced approach to their interactions with children and families with refugee and asylum-seeker backgrounds. This book is structured to allow the reader space to reflect, to consider how

DOI: 10.4324/9781003404231-1

relevant some of the ideas may be in their own contexts, and to contemplate the principles which allow their professional actions to make a difference.

Of necessity, there are limitations. Only five English-speaking countries are represented. There are many other countries whose early carers and educators could have easily made a significant contribution to a much larger research project and a much heftier volume. Nor was there the space or background information to investigate how each of the participant actions could be customised to make a difference in other contexts of caring and early education. However, it is hoped that the following chapters create discussion, facilitate enquiry, and bring some useful information to those who work in the field and contribute to the benefit of these children, their families, and their societies in general.

Chapter 1 provides a very short summary of the current refugee situation. It indicates the steep rise in refugee numbers in the last two years and events that have predicated this increase. As many of the world's areas of crises have been ongoing and featured extensively in the media, attention has been turned to the current numbers in refugee camps, many of which are geographically placed in desolate areas within the boundaries of countries whose economic situations cannot possibly provide them with anything but the most meagre attempts at basic human needs. The chapter content also indicates a number of 'hotspots' around the world which are presenting reasons for international concern about the safety of their populations.

Chapter 2 provides some information about the impact of trauma on babies, toddlers, and young students. It defines what is meant by trauma, complex trauma (CT), and complex childhood trauma (CCT). It explores, in some detail, the ways in which infants and the very young can express symptoms of their experiences without language and explains the possible impact of degrees of trauma on the developmental timelines of children with refugee and asylum-seeker backgrounds, including the ways in which the damage caused can impact as lifelong conditions. It identifies how carers and educators can help recognise behaviours which are indicative of trauma experiences and also alerts these carers and educators how the impact of the tragic circumstances of children in their care can affect them psychologically as vicarious trauma.

Chapter 3 explores the entire notion of the nature of inclusion at all levels of education and care. It discusses systemic, institutional, and individual inclusion and questions the concept of inclusive practices by interrogating the principles underpinning these activities and the criteria by which they are labelled 'inclusive' or not.

Chapter 4 introduces the complex nature of the cultural dimensions of childhood which impact on the ways that children and families interact with each other, maintain social relationships, and communicate effectively in diverse contexts. It examines some of the cultural practices that are not acceptable in the new homelands in which many families with refugee experiences are based, most especially those which are unlawful and likely to cause some retribution from authorities. It examines theories of cultural difference and reminds the readers that the sum total of any society and culture are individuals who have distinct traditions, characteristics, and family tradition which are unique.

Chapter 5 focuses on play. The differences in cultural norms and values may be interpreted through the different perceptions of play that are expressed by the parents in conversation with the participants. A detailed description of play in its various iterations and stages are discussed and its role in society as a positive developmental activity for children is provided. Additionally, the foundational cultural beliefs about the value of play in diverse communities are investigated.

Chapter 6 brings together the emotional, social, and cognitive. It briefly discusses the ancient connections that were believed to exist between these areas of development and explores the notion of intelligence in relation to theories of emotional and social development. It explores the major theorists in social and emotion research and introduces the notion of *salutogenesis*. It returns to the difficulties associated with trauma and cognitive development, alongside the dichotomies of developing social and emotional skills in contexts where these are perceived differently by carers and educators, and the parents of the children in their care.

Chapter 7 provides a detailed insight into the notion of intergenerational trauma. This may be underestimated or simply ignored by many individuals with refugee experiences as the cultural considerations or attitudes to issues of mental health may significantly affect their participation and successful outcomes in trauma-related interventions and service opportunities. It investigates the possible social and emotional attitudes, behaviours, and perspectives that may permeate family and community interactions and the ways in which these can be transferred to their children, including babies *in utero*. It also indicates the extent to which research has established trauma can modify genetic profiles, affecting several generations in families and communities.

Chapter 8 deals with complexities, expectations, and responsibilities that are embedded in the transitioning to school process. It identifies and defines the major characteristics of Western, neoliberalised education and the implications that these have for children from other social and cultural backgrounds, examining the ways in which these education systems often pervert the principles of healthy development in cognition and social and emotional skills in favour of compliance, conventionality, and practices of economy and accountability.

Chapter 9 offers an insight into the authors and their perspectives on some major aspects of the research reported and investigated in this book. As each author in turn prepares and presents one of the three topics under which the subject matter is collated, the remaining authors are invited to join and discuss their thinking around the concerns raised. Serving as a summative chapter to the work, this section illustrates the high value the authors place on the quality and work of early childhood carers and educators while drawing on their own practical experiences and theoretical understandings.

Chapter 1

Diaspora, current challenges, and concerns for the future

Introduction

Each day in preschools, day care centres, and playgroups around the world, educators are welcoming young children and their families with refugee or asylum-seeker experiences. These families were forcibly displaced from their homes by wars or conflicts, famine, or natural disasters and then may have spent years living in refugee camps. Their experiences are often marked with loss, violence, and a resulting trauma that doesn't end when they arrive in their host country. For many families, coming to a new country means learning a different language, deciphering an unusual culture, navigating new expectations, and entering a foreign education system. The teachers, staff members, and administrators who greet these families and care for their young children are among the first responders critical for successful integration.

In all fields, knowledge is at the core of effective practice. While this book takes the reader into playgroups, preschools, and day care centres and addresses some of the most pertinent issues in supporting families with refugee backgrounds, this first chapter provides an understanding of world events and the reasons why so many families are migrating to new lands.

Diaspora

Diaspora has become common usage for many people. Formerly only a familiar term for those interested in the Bible perhaps or those involved in linguistics, the current situation of 117 million people who are displaced or stateless (International Rescue Committee, 2023) across the world has brought this Greek term into everyone's conversations. In 2022, the number of people displaced by war was recorded as 84 million (Sellars et al., 2023). Tragically, world events have increased the number by more than 30 million.

UNICEF estimates that among this total, there are an estimated 43.3 million children, many of whom have been refugees for their entire childhoods. The number of children forcibly displaced from their homes has doubled in

DOI: 10.4324/9781003404231-2

the last decade. The war in Ukraine by itself is responsible for more than 2 million children being forced to flee the country, some with their families, and some alone.

Of the 43.3 million children who were forcibly displaced by the end of 2022, almost 60% (25.8 million) were internally displaced by conflict and violence. The number of refugee and asylum-seeking children also hit a new record of 17.5 million, not including those newly displaced in 2023, including by the conflict in Sudan. In addition, extreme weather events, such as the Pakistan floods and droughts in the Horn of Africa and in the NCA (North of Central America) zone, led to another 12 million displacements of children over the course of 2022 (Ingram, 2023).

The share of refugees who are younger than 18 varies somewhat by region. In Latin America, one in five migrants are children, and in Africa, one in four migrants are children, while the share of refugees who are children is lower in Europe and Oceania (Migration Data Portal, 2021).

Ongoing crises leading to the diaspora

Critical events worldwide, including wars and famine, are contributing to the global diaspora. Of note, in February 2022, Russia launched an invasion of Ukraine, starting the largest ground war in Europe since World War II. In the subsequent 18 months, tens of thousands of Russian and Ukrainian soldiers and thousands of Ukrainian civilians have been killed and another massive global refugee crisis has unfolded (Pavlova et al., 2022). To date, 8 million Ukrainians have been dislocated within the country, 5.8 million Ukrainian refugees have fled to countries across Europe, and an additional 400,000 have sought safety beyond Europe (UNHCR, 2023a). This migration has primarily involved children, mothers, and other adult women as Ukraine's President Volodymyr Zelenskyy declared martial law shortly after the invasion and forbade men between the ages of 18 and 60 from leaving Ukraine. For these refugee families, the traumas of war and relocation have been compounded with this separation from fathers and husbands. In addition to the mental and physical suffering of the Ukrainian refugees, the chaos of 6 million human beings seeking shelter, safety, and some semblance of life in other countries has also had a detrimental effect on the mental health of civilian populations in host countries across Europe. This may be particularly true in countries that have a history of conflicts or invasion with Russia or the former Soviet Republic, where the vicarious trauma of supporting massive numbers of refugees has led to elevated levels of concern, anxiety, and depression across the populace (Massag, et al., 2023). As Ukraine is one of the world's top producers of grain, the outcome of the war is particularly concerning for global food security. Among other reasons, this fact has led numerous countries to support Ukraine with military and humanitarian aid and likely ensures the end to the conflict is nowhere in sight (Reddy, 2023). Unfortunately, the death toll on both sides will continue to climb and the number of refugees will certainly grow. This aggression which has caused so much human disaster has also impacted on the stability of neighbouring Armenia and Azerbaijan, whose two-year-old peace pact appears to be breaking down (International Crisis Group, 2023).

Outside Europe, tensions appear to be rising again in Iran, where the brutal execution of many young people, including children, and the imprisonment and torture of many more who have protested against the strict Islamic regime, in particular the compulsory wearing of the hijab, has alarmed human rights supporters worldwide. Complicated by its increase in uranium supply and nuclear weapons plans, the unrest may cause the regime to tighten its laws even more rigorously and provide a catalyst for increasingly determined protest. The uneasy truce in Yemen where rebels have been challenging the officially recognised government is causing fears the pact may implode at any moment, creating an increase in displacement numbers and further the refugee crisis. A similar situation is being watched in Ethiopia, where international observers have identified atrocities on both sides, most particularly from the Eritreans, with rape used consistently as a weapon of war to terrify and humiliate the civilian population, an estimated 385,000–600,000 of whom were killed in August 2022. The Democratic Republic of the Congo is also poised to resume the horrors of previous conflicts as rebels are systematically devastating the eastern regions of the country, displacing thousands of people. Climate change and Jihadist groups of rebels are creating havoc in the group of countries known as the Sahel. Predominantly an agricultural area, the crop failures due to unfavourable weather conditions have intensified the precarious stability of the region and may increase the numbers by millions of displaced people who may seek to escape from places such as Burkina Faso, Mali, Chad, Niger and Sudan. In other parts of the world, Haiti's gang terror, rape and violence have exacerbated the unrest about the cost of living, the abolition of workers' rights, the dire plight of half the population suffering from starvation and lack of local resources to confine an outbreak of cholera has destabilised an already shaky government and significantly impacted on the populace, a situation described as a 'humanitarian tragedy.' The parliamentary crisis in Pakistan, coupled with recent extensive flooding has intensified the unrest in the country. Taiwan's ongoing separation from China, and the role played by the US in maintaining this division, continues to produce global anxiety by Taiwan's continuing separation from China and the role played by the US in maintaining this division, at least temporarily (International Crisis Group, 2023).

Meanwhile, close to a million people in Central America have been forced to leave their homes in order to escape gang violence. Many more have been displaced multiple times within their own countries or have been deported back home, often into dangerous situations. All of this is made worse by political instability and poverty, famine and drought, and the economic and social impacts of COVID-19. Political turmoil in Nicaragua since 2018 has forced some 200,000 people to flee persecution and human rights abuses. In the 'North of Central America' region – comprising El Salvador, Guatemala, and Honduras – gang violence, political turmoil, extortion, persecution, and sexual violence have forced hundreds of thousands of people to flee their homes in search of safety and a better life. This political, economic, and social instability is compounded by a multi-year drought affecting the 'Dry Corridor' running through Honduras, Guatemala, and El Salvador. The drought has led to a crippling rise in hunger. Additionally, an estimated 1.5 million people in the region have been displaced by Hurricanes Eta and Iota, two of the most powerful storms to hit Central America in decades.

Colombia has seen more than 40 years of conflict that has raged between the Colombian government, guerrilla groups, paramilitaries, and narco-traffickers. These wars have led to an estimated 50,000–200,000 fatalities and have displaced millions of others. According to the United Nations High Commissioner for Refugees (UNHCR), there are currently 3.5 million displaced persons inside Colombia, and another 500,000–750,000 are seeking refuge in neighbouring countries. The crisis in Columbia is the largest displacement crisis in the Western Hemisphere and constitutes one of the largest refugee populations in the world. Meanwhile, in Venezuela political and economic crises have driven more than 7 million people from their homes since 2015 (roughly a quarter of the national population). The overwhelming majority (about 6 million) of these refugees have relocated to nearby countries.

The crisis in South Sudan created as the country became newly independent has forced over 4 million to flee their homes, many of those leaving the country have fled to neighbouring African countries some of which are experiencing their own refugee evacuations. These include the Democratic Republic of Congo, which, while hosting refugees from other countries, is still adding to the diaspora with 909,000 of its citizens currently estimated as displaced as the result of the 25-year conflict, the ongoing nature of which causes numbers of evacuees to increase steadily each year. A similar situation exists in Sudan. While offering refuge to refugees from other countries, Sudan itself also contributes approximately 850,000 individuals to the displaced population in Africa. Protracted violence and persecution in the Central African Republic and Eritrea have resulted in another 738,000 and 501,000 refugees, respectively (Concern, 2023).

In addition to the 36 million people seeking new homelands, there are approximately 5.4 million asylum seekers who cannot remain in their countries of origin for fear of persecution, death, torture, or other retaliatory actions against themselves and their families (UNHCR, 2023). Asylum seekers differ from refugees in only one aspect, they have not been formally recognised as refugees by their host country. In addition to the major crisis locations across the world, there are many minority groups who are seeking refuge and who may remain stateless for decades. These include the Karana people of Madagascar, the Roma and other ethnic minorities of the former Yugoslav Republic of Macedonia, the Pemba of Kenya, and the Makonde of Kenya in addition to minority groups across Asia and the Middle Eastern countries (UNHCR, 2017).

Refugee journeys and refugee camps

The majority of refugees end up in countries that border their own and one in five refugees live in refugee camps of one type or another, where they may live for years or even decades waiting to be resettled. Many of these camps are managed by countries and relief agencies, but more than 2 million individuals live in self-settled camps (UNHCR, 2023). Existing refugee camps have been expanded and newer sites have sprung up in various locations where previously there was little or no human habitation or where borders meet, and immigration officials dominate the possibility of newcomers entering the countries. Sadly, the largest of these are situated in some of the poorest countries. Bangladesh hosts the world's largest refugee camp, with 880,000 Rohingya refugees who have fled from Myanmar due to persistent persecution. About 200,000 people from South Sudan, Sudan, Somalia, the Democratic Republic of the Congo (DRC), Burundi, Ethiopia, and Uganda are housed in the Kakuma Refugee Camp in a desert region of Kenya. A second Kenyan camp complex is home to over 200,000 people mainly from Somalia, and the influx of new arrivals is constant. Jordan is home to the fourth largest camp, Za'atari Refugee Camp which 'houses' 80,000 people, the majority of whom are from the neighbouring country of Syria and who make up 25% of the world's refugee population as the ten-year war relentlessly continues to devastate communities and country. The conflict and persecution in Afghanistan continue and 10% of all refugees worldwide are Afghans, the majority of whom are confined to camps in Pakistan and Iran.

The refugee populations who reside in these camps are almost continually at risk. There is widespread disease amongst the occupants which is created and exacerbated by lack of hygienic facilities, shortage of freshwater, and adequate food supplies and climatic conditions. Added to this are stories of abuse, exploitation, and maltreatment. Organised educational programmes may exist for some groups of residents, but language, religious, and other cultural considerations may easily limit these opportunities to specific cohorts of children and young adults. These conditions may be exaggerated in self-founded camps as the organised and managed camps are regulated more effectively, but they may also be subjected to multiple restrictions, which may result in people residing in camps for more than 25 years – a situation which has the potential to create additional trauma and increase the probability of intergenerational trauma. These conditions may also apply to the 62.5 million people who are internally displaced in their respective countries, as they are also vulnerable and without the resources that they would access as part of their everyday lives.

Host countries in the West

As the number of refugees continues to grow, it seems the numbers of places of relative safety and protection are dwindling. The great majority of refugees are currently being accepted into poor and middle-income countries (with the exception of Germany that has accepted more than 2 million in the past few years). Unfortunately, in many Western, English-speaking countries, there has been a rise in anti-immigrant sentiment and political movements of late. These movements have played on public fears of broken borders, worries about terrorism, anti-Muslim and racist beliefs, and economic concerns about competing for jobs and finite government benefits (CFR, 2023).

Taking the United States as an example, under President Trump, the country dramatically lowered the number of refugees it accepted annually by more than 80%. During the 2016 Presidential election, the then candidate Donald Trump repeatedly criticised his opponent for her stance on taking in additional Syrian refugees and in an infamous phone call with the then Prime Minister Malcolm Turnbull, Trump stated, 'I hate taking refugees, I guarantee you they are bad. That is why they are in prison right now. They are not going to be wonderful people' (The Guardian, 2017).

With the election of President Biden in 2020, the United States has slowly started increasing refugee resettlement. More refugees arrived in the United States in the first eight months of 2023 than any year since 2017. The Biden Administration also advanced new policies to expand protection for nationals of Cuba, Haiti, Nicaragua, and Venezuela, as well as for displaced Afghans and Ukrainians (Ward & Batalova, 2023). Nationals of the DRC, Myanmar (also known as Burma), and Syria made up almost 60% of refugee arrivals to the United States in 2022. Conversely, refugee resettlement from Latin America and the Caribbean has been consistently low despite the growing need for humanitarian protection for persecuted peoples in these regions (Ward & Batalova, 2023).

While the chances for refugees seeking to relocate to the United States under the current administration have improved, the country took in just 25,000 refugees in 2022. In that same year, Australia received less than 20,000 refugees, England accepted 23,000, New Zealand accepted 1,500, and Northern Ireland accepted less than 1,000 (UNHCR, 2023). In the pages that follow, educators from each of these countries offer insights about how they welcome and meet the needs of the children and families with refugee experiences whom they serve.

Conclusion

In the face of the diaspora, when looking at the massive numbers of people fleeing crises and flowing across borders, it can be easy to lose sight of the fact that behind these numbers are individual human beings, each with unique experiences, values, and desires. These numbers represent men, women, children, and infants who didn't choose to flee their homes, leave behind their extended families, and all of their possessions and the only world they have ever known. These numbers are families that have arrived in new lands seeking safety, security, and belonging.

Standing ready to meet these families and their young children arriving as part of these waves of new immigrants are the early childhood educators who staff childcare and early learning centres in countries around the world. The following chapters will offer insight into the vital work of these early childhood educators and the ways they have created opportunities to welcome and integrate newly arrived children and families.

References

CFR. (2023). *The world's swelling refugee population has shrinking options*. Council on Foreign Relations. https://www.cfr.org/refugee-crisis/

Concern. (2023). *The 10 largest refugee crisis in 2023*. Retrieved September 17, 2023, from https://www.concern.net/news/largest-refugee-crises

Ingram, T. (2023). *Number of displaced children reaches new high of 43.3 million*. UNICEF. https://www.unicef.org/press-releases/number-displaced-children-reaches-new-high-433-million#:~:text=UNICEF%2FUN0609795%2F2022%206%2D,to%20the%20Ukrainian%2DSlovak%20border.&text=NEW%20YORK%2C%2014%20June%202023,them%20for%20their%20entire%20childhood

International Crisis Group. (2023). *10 Conflicts to watch in 2023*. https://www.crisis-group.org/global/10-conflicts-watch-2023#ukraine

International Rescue Committee. (2023). *Refugee crisis*. Retrieved September 17, 2023, from https://www.rescue.org/topic/refugee-crisis-100-million-displaced#:~:text=There%20are%20now%20more%20than,offices%20in%20the%20United%20States

Massag, J., Diexer, S., Klee, B., Costa, D., Gottschick, C., Broda, A., Purschke, O., Opel, N., Binder, M., Sedding, D., Frese, T., Girndt, M., Hoell, J., Moor, I., Rosendahl, J., Gekle, M., & Mikolajczyk, R. (2023). Anxiety, depressive symptoms, and distress over the course of the war in Ukraine in three federal states in Germany. Frontiers in psychiatry, 14, 1167615. https://doi.org/10.3389/fpsyt.2023.1167615

Migration Data Portal. (2021). *Child and young migrants*. https://www.migrationda-taportal.org/themes/child-and-young-migrants

Pavlova, I., Graf-Vlachy, L., Petrytsa, P., Wang, S., & Zhang, S. X. (2022). Early evidence on the mental health of Ukrainian civilian and professional combatants during the Russian invasion. European Psychiatry, 65(1), e79.

Sellars, M., Imig, S., & Fischetti, J. (2023). *Creating spaces of wellbeing and belonging for refugee and asylum-seeker students: Skills and strategies for classroom teachers*. Routledge. https://doi.org/10.4324/9781003207900

Reddy, M. (2023, March 2). What history shows: How will the war in Ukraine end?. Al Jazeera. https://www.aljazeera.com/features/2023/3/2/what-history-shows-how-will-the-war-in-ukraine-end

The Guardian. (2017, August 4). *"Local milk people": Donald Trump's odd expression inspires memes.* https://www.theguardian.com/us-news/2017/aug/04/local-milk-people-donald-trumps-odd-expression-inspires-memes

UNHCR. (2017). *This is our home: Stateless minorities and their search for citizenship.* Retrieved September 17, 2023, from https://www.unhcr.org/ibelong/wp-content/uploads/UNHCR_EN2_2017IBELONG_Report_ePub.pdf

UNHCR. (2023a). *Figures at a glance.* Retrieved September 17, 2023, from https://www.unhcr.org/au/about-unhcr/who-we-are/figures-glance

UNHCR. (2023b). *Displacement in Central America.* Retrieved September 18, 2023, from https://www.unhcr.org/emergencies/displacement-central-america

UNHCR. (2023c). *Columbia situation.* Retrieved September 18, 2023, from https://reporting.unhcr.org/operational/situations/colombia-situation#:~:text=Throughout%202022%2C%20UNHCR%20directly%20assisted,and%20services%2C%20including%20humanitarian%20assistance

Ward, N. & J. Batalova. (2023). Refugees and asylees in the United States. SPOTLIGHT. Migration Policy Institute. Retrieved September 18, 2023, from https://www.migrationpolicy.org/article/refugees-and-asylees-united-states#:~:text=Over%20the%2043%20years%20of,were%20granted%20in%20FY%201994

Chapter 2

The impact of trauma on the well-being and development of babies and young children

Introduction

Creating environments where the youngest children feel happy and safe can be challenging for any early education provider. For educators serving children with refugee and asylum-seeker experiences, children who have experienced forced displacement, the loss of home, pets, or even family members, the work is much more challenging. This chapter delves into the far-reaching consequences of trauma, its impact on the youngest learners, and the caustic effects of vicarious trauma on those who support and educate newly arrived families.

What is trauma?

Understanding trauma is complex. It becomes even more complex when the trauma sufferers are babies, toddlers, and young children whose language skills are insufficiently developed to successfully share their perceptions and personal responses to the events or circumstances that have created this trauma. In this context, the trauma experiences that are being discussed are those associated with circumstances or events that cause extreme emotional distress. Although it can be argued that everyone suffers from some kind of emotional trauma throughout their lifetimes, it is the complexity of multiple traumatic episodes, the severity of the distress experienced, and the duration of the episodes that distinguish the impact of these stressful encounters on adults, young people, and children, including babies. It refers to an event or events that are psychologically overwhelming, irrespective of whether the threat is real or perceived. Complex trauma is associated with multiple sources of trauma that may be experienced simultaneously or with an ongoing psychologically overwhelming event that is experienced over a longer duration. There are many causes of trauma, several of which are experienced by communities with refugee and asylum-seeker experiences. Included in these are several which have been encountered by these communities. Exposure to episodes of violence, war, and death (Aviles et al., 2006; Betancourt et al., 2012), including violence in the home, neglect and maltreatment (De Bellis, 2005; Twardosz & Lutzker,

DOI: 10.4324/9781003404231-3

2010), displacement (Dryden-Peterson, 2017), poverty (Payne, 2001), and cultural and social misalignment and differences may be traumatic for families before and during their journeys and on arrival in their new homelands (Arar et al., 2019; Edgeworth, 2013; Steimel, 2016; Stewart & Mulvey, 2013). While cultural and social interpretations of what constitutes many of these events may vary, the key to understanding trauma lies in the degree to which the experiences cause the individual to feel psychologically overwhelmed, the chemical and hormonal changes the events create, and their subsequent impact on the brain functioning of the individual (Ziegler, 2011), which, in turn, is expressed as observable behaviours (McLean, 2016; Schore, 2015).

As with all experiences, commonly used terms have the potential to more accurately describe the degree to which the events have impacted on the successful, everyday functioning of those who have encountered overwhelming psychological occurrences. Adverse childhood experiences (ACEs) (Felitti et al., 1998), such as exposure to one or more of the factors detailed above, may have negative consequences for the developmental progress of children's cognitive and socio-emotional skills (Aviles et al., 2006; Blodgett & Lanigan, 2018; Sellars et al., 2022). A single source of trauma may also be referred to simply as childhood trauma (CT) (Briere et al., 2001). The impact of these experiences, identified also as complex childhood trauma (CCT) (McDonald et al., 2014), goes beyond the individual and may lead to the social exclusion of entire communities as the result of 'poverty, inequity and decent work' (Yang et al., 2016, p. 33–53), conditions which are often found in refugee and asylum-seeker communities, rendering the environments in which their children are raised to be characterised by ongoing stress, discrimination, and economic restrictions, identified as traumatic stress or toxic stress. As these aspects of trauma include multiple alterations to the development and effective functioning of the brain due to the resultant high levels of cortisol (Alayarian, 2018; Chen et al., 2009; Montgomery, 2010; Scheeringa & Zeanah, 2001; Teicher et al., 2003; Weiland et al., 2014; Weiss, 2007), traumatic stress is associated with delayed skill development and poor school performance. Many of the difficulties experienced in learning contexts, including those that promote socio-emotional development for young children, can be attributed to their exposure to situations that create toxic stress, also known as traumatic stress, which are further identified as ACEs. This is because they have the potential to impact negatively on chemical balances and neural systems that regulate human development and growth (Alayarian, 2018; Chen et al., 2009; Gao et al., 2015; Teicher et al., 2003; Twardosz & Lutzker, 2010). The outward expressions of these biological and psychological changes can be observed as socio-emotional behaviours, physical symptoms, and affective and cognitive signs of delay or regression in expected development. This has given rise to a relatively new construct developmental trauma disorder (DTD) which describes an array of trauma symptoms in babies, toddlers, and young children created by continued exposure to violent events coupled with inadequate care giving (Stolbach et al., 2013).

Research findings

Nearly every participant we interviewed talked of the very present and both dramatic and subtle impacts of trauma exhibited by newly arrived children and their families. A resettlement director in the United States and a preschool director in Australia shared stories of individuals dealing with the effects of unimaginable grief, loss, and fear and the ways educators respond.

> *Context:* The children are from six weeks to six years and we are located in the same building as the English college. The mothers come and learn English on-site in the level upstairs and their children come to us. Most of our families are Afghan refugees, so they make up 90% of our families here. Once they've arrived through the Settlement Service, they're set up with housing, everything that they need, and of course, English classes. The other families we have are Syrian, and a lot of Ukrainians are coming. We also have Russian, Japanese, and the Solomon Islands speakers, so a big, broad range of families.

> We find out things that work all the time for families; we often find little triggers that might just help families, such as turning the lights out. You know these children often become very afraid of that. We found that they were told to remain silent in the dark. If you know this, something is happening outside. So, we have to be aware of lights and noises.... It's things such as cars backfiring. We're on a main road here in Mollybrook, oh and the fire alarm. There are lots of triggers so that we can prepare the families for these things, even down to this is what the fire alarm sounds like, and I've had a conversation with the building manager and said, could we have a fire drill today? At this time, I warn families. This is what it sounds like. This is what it means. This is what we're going to do because we often don't realize that these things can be very confronting for families.

> *Context:* I have been with this non-profit for more than a decade. We resettle a lot of families from the Democratic Republic of Congo, from Burundi, Rwanda, Tanzania. Some of our other families are from Afghanistan or Iraq or a few of the other places that we have resettled from Nepal. Transportation and getting children to school is really challenging for these families. Families receive temporary cash assistance, but it ends quickly and parents need to find employment first.

> I think that when we look at that demographic of new immigrants to this community, recently resettled, often times we try to let our volunteers and our partners just know about the layers of loss that our families are experiencing. It could be physical loss and death in their family, loss of their home, their country but also just culture and traditions and their profession. We often times work with families that have been professors in their home country or doctors or dentists and their credentials don't

translate and now they are working in a warehouse here or different entry level jobs. And so there is layers of loss and grief that families are processing on top of culture shocks and cultural adjustments and then there is also this thing that happens that when families have been living in survival mode for so long and they have finally reached this level of stability, all of those things that they have suppressed, all of that trauma, all of that loss, all of that grief comes out and manifests itself in lots of different ways.

And so we can see this in parents and adults kind of in your different typical coping ways like anxiety and depression, night terrors and things like that. But, in children it can come out in tummy issues, behavior and kind of what we would typically label as ADHD or different things like that. Like they are also processing and experiencing these things as well as their process of resettlement and adjustment to their new country is really traumatic in on itself. And so for educators or caregivers or support systems for us to have kind of just a level of awareness and kind of empathy as we are engaging with our families and realizing I might be dealing with a symptom that doesn't have anything to do with the root.

Unique contexts, global principles

Despite working on opposite sides of the planet, each of our participants shared similar stories of families experiencing the effects of trauma and the need to continually gather information and modify practice. Our Australian director proactively identifies triggers in and around her classroom that may upset her young children, eliminating those she can and educating about those beyond her control. The realisation that a dark room equates to danger for many of her students or that a loud noise in the street elicits terrifying memories of violence compels her to be proactive. Our American resettlement director talked of the need to educate teachers, volunteers, and the broader community to the complexity of trauma, its causes, and the ways it can manifest itself. While she is keenly aware of the debilitating effects the loss of family members, homes, and property can have on individuals, she also cautioned about the less obvious impact the loss of status and diminished perception of self-worth can have on adults. She also worries about the well-being of young children returning home to parents wrestling with such realities and related emotions. This participant also highlighted how trauma can manifest differently for adults and children. She reports the parents she has worked with experience of depression, anxiety, and troubles sleeping while young students often present with stomach aches, irritability, and troubles concentrating. Importantly, she reminds us that symptoms are often unexpected and inconsistent. Each of our participants places a premium on knowing all they can about the vulnerable families with whom they work.

Creating environments where triggers are minimised, and children and families are understood is important and requires educators to be empowered and well informed about the complexities of trauma. As the body of research presented at the outset of this chapter indicates, individuals who have experienced complex trauma are likely to exhibit a myriad of symptoms that may or may not seem linked to their experiences and educators need to be mindful of the continued presence of trauma as concerns arise. The unimaginable experience of being forced from your home, losing your possessions and livelihood, fleeing to a refugee camp, and then landing in a foreign land with little support is, as Ziegler (2011) asserts, most likely to impact brain functioning. Among our youngest children, complex trauma can affect physical and mental well-being and negatively impact learning and academic development. For children with refugee backgrounds, it is important that teachers support developmental delays, physical maladies, and behavioural issues, but it is imperative they are cautious about not assigning labels or diagnoses that might limit the forward potential of these young learners.

Trauma and the young

Children are particularly vulnerable to the impact of trauma. Childhood is a critical time for development. From birth onwards, the developmental process that began *in utero* continues at a rapid rate in all areas of growth. Children exposed to trauma in the early years are at risk of developing multiple problems, with their vulnerability being exacerbated by their lack of capacities to fend for themselves, unlike many other, older children. These may be physical health problems, emotional and behavioural issues, and impaired cognition (Barowsky & McIntyre, 2010; Coulter & Mooney, 2018; Hart, 2009; Romano et al., 2015). Refugee and asylum-seeking children are particularly vulnerable as they frequently have had exposure to violence, war, loss, and other significantly traumatic events (Mace et al., 2014; Vervliet et al., 2014). Because of this probability of multiple traumatic experiences, many children are experiencing CCT in addition to the ACE of displacement (Frater-Mathieson, 2004; Oberg, 2019), which, for many, is only one of three events that may be traumatic. Children who have CCT may exhibit many symptoms of psychological distress, including, but not limited to, withdrawal, unreasonable fears, distress at being left alone, nightmares, recurrence of traumatic images, hyper-anxiety, insomnolence, concentration difficulties, and lack of agency and enjoyment in their lives (Fazel & Stein, 2002 p. 367). These findings were confirmed by the more recent studies of Sapmaz et al. (2017) and Alayarian (2018). Sadly, because of the environments and experiences of family members, these behaviours are frequently complicated by malnutrition, poverty, and lack of parental or caregiver support (Davidson, Skull, Burgner, et al., 2004; Davidson, Skull, Chaney, et al., 2004). Consequently, it is not surprising that students with these experiences and subsequent symptoms do not achieve well academically, they have attachment issues and difficulties with executive function capacities such as regulation of emotion (Romano et al., 2015; Sellars, 2010).

Despite the acknowledgement of the long-term impacts of CCT, Fraser et al. (2019) indicate that there are few screening tools for traumatised children aged 0–3 years and that consequently this group are underrepresented in the welfare systems. This is despite the understanding that trauma-affected babies and toddlers may develop complex psychological disorders if early identification and intervention measures are not put in place to support them. As children at this age are not fully verbal, their identification frequently relies heavily on behavioural cues. Like their older counterparts, traumatised babies and toddlers may exhibit symptoms of excessive clinginess, may demonstrate excessive crying, aggression and regressive behaviours, sleeplessness and irritability, digestive and eating problems or, conversely, be totally withdrawn and be unresponsive to stimuli. They may also be hypervigilant, startling easily, and fear adults they connect to the traumatic events. The difficulty lies in the identification of trauma-related symptoms as indictive of these events as, observed singly or in combination with select others, these behaviours may be indicative of multiple other infant-related disorders, most especially when the symptoms may range from extreme and intense to subtle and intermittent. The identification of trauma-related behaviours in the three- to six-year-old age groups is less problematic (Fraser et al., 2019). This is because they have more sophisticated language and communication skills. They can discuss their feelings, describe where they may be hurting, and share their worries and fears. These children may exhibit somewhat different symptoms of trauma. They may retell the traumatic event repeatedly and replicate the event in their play, complain of bodily aches and pains, and display regressive behaviours such as bed wetting when they had previously been consistently continent, or having frequent 'accidents' when they had formerly been observed to have been reliably toilet trained. They may also be observably fearful and anxious. One of the findings of Frazer et al.'s study which highlighted the importance of parental and/or caregiver relationship with the child was the importance of the parental report which was designed to capture the child's pattern of behaviours that were of concern. Parents who were suffering trauma or mental health issues themselves appeared to find the reflection required to complete the report difficult. This is a salient finding for many refugee and asylum-seeking children whose entire families have been subjected to traumatic events which may then impact on their capacities to adequately care for their children.

While incidents of infants fearing the adults they associate with the traumatic events and toddlers replaying the traumatic episodes in their play or repetitive storytelling may be distressing to observe, the opposite reaction may be more damaging to the child themselves. Disassociation with the event may have long-term impact and result in serious psychological damage (Alayarian, 2018). Literature about dissociative disorder in young children indicate that research is still in the early stages; however, it appears that be-haviours may include

> both auditory and visual hallucinations, conversations with imaginary friends or family members who might have been killed, unexplained ritual behaviour, unusual changes in patterns of eating and sleeping, or fluctuat-ing academic and intellectual performance.
>
> (Alayarian, 2018, p. 42)

The prognosis for children suffering from dissociative disorder which is not addressed and treated is not encouraging. It appears that these behaviours may lead to neurological disturbances expressed as psychosis-like symptoms and personality disorders such as schizophrenia. Stolbach et al. (2013) explored the symptoms of children suffering from CCT, finding that many of them were not captured by their diagnostic tool designed to identify post-traumatic stress disorder (PTSD), leading them to record and identify these symptoms under the banner of DTD. This disorder was characterised by

> pervasive dysregulation of (a) affective and physiological systems, (b) atten-tional and behavioural systems, and (c) self and relational systems.
>
> (Stolbach et al., 2013, p. 484)

These developmental disruptions were because of exposure to repeated epi-sodes of violence in addition to severe, repeated emotional abuse and repeated separation from caregivers or repeated change of caregivers which occur in the first few years of life and continue. The children who participated in the study exhibited lack of normal developmental attributes in the following areas: af-fective and physiological dysregulation, attentional and behavioural dysregula-tion, and self and dysregulation (Stolbach et al., 2013, pp. 488–489).

Without intervention and support, limited development in the three areas can cause considerable disruption to these children in every area of their lives as they grow and become adults. Trauma alters the brain by regulating hormones, particularly cortisol and neurotransmitters, which affect brain development, particularly stress-induced modifications on the infant's brain during a sensi-tive period on postnatal development (Teicher et al., 2003 p. 167). Develop-mental delays found in children as the result of traumatic experiences are well documented in children (see, for example, Alayarian, 2018; Mares & Jureidini, 2004). Continual exposure to trauma in infancy or childhood can result in 'the failure to develop essential neurological structures necessary for the infant's healthy development' (Alayarian, 2018, p. 23). For younger children, PTSD and other trauma symptoms are often expressed through re-enacting play be-haviours. They repeat themes of the trauma they have experienced, playing fighting games and re-enacting traumatic events (Alayarian, 2018; Stolbach et al., 2013). Their play may be more violent and aggressive with toy guns.

They may pretend to shoot and kill other children (Theisen-Womersley, 2021; Womersley, 2021). Although very young children and toddlers may not display these symptoms, refugee and asylum-seeking children who have been consistently exposed to traumatic events may be observed demonstrating clinging behaviour, thumb sucking, baby talking, temper tantrums, and bedwetting, and, as previously noted, may lose an acquired development skill such as toilet training, talking, or walking (Alayarian, 2018). In a small study, all eight children aged one to four years experienced behavioural problems such as 'frequent crying, food refusal, and requiring nappies having previous acquired bladder control' (Lorek et al., 2009 p. 622).

Research findings

Multiple participants in our research shared anecdotes about the unexpected ways trauma can affect the youngest children. Two preschool directors from large American cities shared insights from their decades of working with newly arrived families.

> *Context:* I've had a lot of experience in different areas, working in the early childhood field, owning and operating my own early childhood centre in [a large mid-western city in the US]. In addition to a diverse student cohort, the centre I owned served families who fled war. I've also been a university faculty member and an endowed university Chair in early childhood education.

> When the bells went off, the kids all hit the floor. Because, in the refugee camp, when the bell goes off, they will be bombed...So, being trauma-informed is not just saying these kids have been through trauma. We know they've been through a trauma. But, it's really thinking about it. Like, do you have bells that will go off? You can't have bells. And, anybody in uniform, the kids would start crying. Things are different, like they may have a child who's 4 or 5 years old and still in diapers, still sucking their thumb. Still, can't drink, can't eat with a fork. Your expectation when you're working with kids who've been through these things, you've got to get rid of all of your expectations. Your ages and stages of development that we all know, that kids should be able to do this, by this time. When you bring in children who have gone through this trauma, how is that affecting their development? Their social and emotional development, and physical development? How is that going to impact what they do within the classroom? Now we also know that kids catch up quickly, and even in that new immigrant centre in the city, they were sending the Pre. K through first-grade kids off after about three months, once they got a little English and understood how school worked. You know, line up here, get your lunch, sit down here, and open a milk carton this way. They got that pretty quick, and they could go

off and do it. So, the younger kids are going to learn it quickly. But being aware of what has happened to them in the past, and once they leave school, that they go home to these depressed, trauma-affected families. You know, being aware of what's happening there.

Context: I was the Director of the Child Development Centre [in a large US city] for 30 years. We just closed our centre last year. We had a large African American population along with immigrant families. It was stressful for parents because at our centre it was at least a year to 18 months wait to get in. Families were already very stressed when they got to our city. The families all took care of each other. It was a village that took care of children.

They're often hoarding. You know they're often eating all kinds of food. You know they're eating tons of food because they've gone for so long without eating. For instance, in our centre, we had a snack station. The snack was put out. There were granola bars that the kids knew when they got up from nap, they went over and got their snack. I've seen situations with children in my center where they've gone over there, and they've taken every last snack bar. That was okay, and we've had to talk with the other children and to them to develop that sense of trust. But the first week, they needed every snack bar. That's what they needed. The piece of that is that you have to have adults that understand that. So how do you provide that training for people who work with children and families? That's where you can draw on the talent of the adult who is the parents of your Bosnian children or your Afghan children, and you ask them to be partners with you in this learning and this understanding.

Unique contexts, global principles

These two American preschool directors offered rich anecdotes and advice about the ways trauma affects the youngest learners. Our first director asserted that being aware of the presence and power of triggers is foundational. Understanding a school bell or the presence of a police officer or soldier can terrify students compels educators to be constantly aware and supportive. This director also advised that we should throw away expectations when it comes to ages and stages of development for children who are grappling with complex trauma. She offered that educators should understand newly arrived children may still be toilet training long after their host peers, or that their social, emotional, and academic development may also be greatly delayed. But she was also clear young children often catch up quickly, that the debilitating consequences of trauma are frequently and rapidly overcome by resilient young learners. Our second director, from a large urban centre, shared the story of newly arrived children hoarding food. She associated this hoarding with students' prior experiences of hunger and her response was to help the other children in the class understand why an individual might feel compelled to hoard. This director also spoke of the imperative to educate the educators in the room to understand the behaviours of newly arrived children. By partnering with parents with refugee backgrounds, she advises, preschools can access contextually appropriate understandings.

Creating welcoming classrooms in which every child feels safe and where the classroom teachers are trusted is complex work. It requires educators to understand trauma and the ways it can affect children. As our research participants highlighted, children dealing with trauma can display academic performance and behaviours that fall outside expected classroom norms. Many of our interviewees talked about the need to be accepting and discuss atypical behaviours, including hoarding or cowering from noises, rather than attempting to change students' actions. Safe environments enable young children to react as they need and, over time, children grow more comfortable and more able to engage like their host peers. But how do you develop knowledgeable early childhood educators capable of responding appropriately? Often the degrees of difference between the experiences of early childhood educators and families with refugee backgrounds are immense. Fortunately, in many cases, the very families being served, and other refugees in the broader community, can offer the insights necessary to build an understanding educator workforce. Preschool and day care staff would be well served by building relationships with the families of their newly arrived students.

Vicarious trauma

Vicarious trauma and its avoidance play a critical role in the work of caregivers and educators in the early years contexts: day care facilities, childminding agencies, preschools, kindergartens, and the first years of schooling. One of the difficulties facing many educators and carers is their predisposition towards empathy for the children and their families. While this is morally and ethically appropriate, the cost of empathy in many cases can be detrimental to the carers themselves (Arar et al., 2018; Cameron et al., 2019), who may not be readily able to disassociate themselves from the suffering and loss that has been endured by those for whom they are responsible. The psychological impact of shared traumatic experiences on others is generally known as vicarious trauma. It may also be described as

> secondary traumatic stress, compassion fatigue, burnout, countertransference, traumatic countertransference, posttraumatic stress disorder, emotional contagion, and shared trauma.
>
> (Branson, 2019, p. 2)

These terms themselves provide a sound indication of the ways in which teachers and caregivers may 'adopt' the trauma of others through their capacities for empathy and compassion. While Marriage and Marriage (2005) found that some degree of vicarious trauma was evident in all the experienced participants of their study, there is a recognised need for strategies and support systems for all those who have to analyse the impact of and work to support survivors of trauma in the professional capacities (Moran & Asquith, 2020).

McCann and Pearlman (1990) provide some clarity on how vicarious trauma can manifest itself in professionals who work with victims of trauma itself. They discuss the notion of professional 'burnout' as individuals displaying the symptoms of depression, of developing attitudes which lack compassion and empathy, who have experienced boredom and a sense of hopelessness with the work in which they are engaged. Those supporting victims of torture may also develop systems of PTSD (Pross, 2006). These psychological indicators not only hinder the work in which these individuals are engaged but have negative implications for their mental health and safety, for which their employers are responsible and are associated with practitioner isolation, feelings of making ambiguous progress in effecting the healing process, continual, non-reciprocal drain on their capacities for empathy and compassion, and failing to live up to their personal and professional expectations. 'Countertransference' may also be the cause of vicarious trauma. In these instances, the traumatic episodes described by those suffering trauma may trigger responses and feelings of un-resolved trauma experienced by the those seeking to support the traumatised children and their families in formal care and educational settings. Finally, the empathy that is felt for those who have suffered traumatic may lead to the car-ers themselves transferring the impacts of the traumatic events to themselves, most especially those individuals who have the capacity for radical empathy (Ratcliffe, 2012).

McCann and Pearlman (1990, pp. 137–138) propose that caring for those who have suffered trauma may impact on the carers' sense of self and percep-tions of the world. They state:

> Janoff-Bulman (1985) asserts that victimizing life events challenge three basic assumptions or beliefs about the self and the world: the belief in per-sonal invulnerability; the view of oneself in a positive light; and the belief in a meaningful, orderly world. Similarly, Taylor and Brown (1988) have reviewed the evidence that illusions about self and world are adaptive and enhance self-esteem and mental health. Epstein (1989) presents four basic assumptions which he asserts are disrupted by trauma. These include the beliefs that the world is benign, the world is meaningful, the self is worthy, and people are trustworthy.

> sparking

While there may exist the view that vicarious trauma is an unavoidable im-pact of working with victims of trauma, such as the case discussed by Arar et al. (2018), there appear to be a number of strategies and processes that help to mitigate the impacts of this experience. Support systems which allow carers and teachers to discuss their feelings without pathologising them, to resolve any emotional responses created by countertransference, to work through their suffering and distress with processes that are similar to those they employ to support the healing of others, and to share their coping strategies with colleagues are among the most helpful approaches for healing vicarious trauma. However, approaches which aim to prevent vicarious trauma, specifically those supporting refugee and asylum-seeking trauma, include carers developing a strong focus on self-observation and self-care, continuing education about research and new approaches to dealing with trauma, skilled supervision and interactions by management teams, and encouraging refugee and asylum-seeking individuals to seek inclusion in a range of general health-care facilities and provisions (Pross, 2006). While organisational factors contributed to vicarious trauma in mental health workers (Sutton et al., 2022), it would be hoped that the organisational structures of caring environments such as schools, nurseries, preschools, and childcare establishments remain sufficiently flexible and well educated to prevent, rather than contribute, to vicarious trauma in its staff. The scoping review conducted by Kim et al. (2022) focused on identifying the most promising interventions for avoiding vicarious trauma in those who cared for victims of trauma. They pinpointed four types of interventions that promised positive outcomes in preventing and managing these psychological impacts. These were interventions that were characterised by a primary focus on education in psychology, those which centred on mindfulness, those which concentrated on art and other recreational programmes, and those which employed therapies from alternative medicines. It appears that current research into this area of health reflects the range of cultural and social diversity that is to be found in the educational and care contexts that support the needs of babies, toddlers, and young children with refugee and asylum-seeker experiences.

Research findings

Working closely with families with refugee experiences can take a massive toll on empathetic and compassionate individuals. Participants in our research talked about the need to provide educators' support to help them process the vicarious trauma they experience. We spoke with a teacher in Northern Ireland who receives regular counselling and a psychologist in the United States who counsels educators working with young refugees.

> *Context:* You know about the troubles here. Our school is located by a very traditionally working-class Protestant community. And now the school. It's about 95%, what they call newcomers. That's the term they use here. It's not my term. All, pretty much all, speak English as their second or third or fourth language. But now we've got more and more refugees from other

parts of the world. Afghanistan, Iran, Iraq, and other African countries like Eritrea and Nigeria, Angola places like that. The turnover of children has really, really increased. My class now is about a third different to what it was when I started the year off. A lot of new faces, a lot of faces gone.

The educational psychologist will give us advice. I have, like a monthly meeting with him as well. And we just chat things through because I hear a lot of traumatic stuff, and it's second hand. You know it does it impact on you. So I get help from him just to chat basically for like an hour every month, and it's great, really helps. That's a great service.

Context: I am working to provide support to the staff and families engaged with a refugee resettlement and empowerment organisation in [mid-size US city]. I am a psychologist and provide reflective consultation to a variety of child serving agencies and, I want to be careful about what I share, but I think it is okay to say that I also work within our early intervention setting.

I want to be careful about any confidentiality. So let me speak generally in the several cases that I am thinking about over the past weeks. So, I provide reflective consultation for either clinicians or early intervention specialists. So, we talk about how it feels to do the work. A lot of times, boundaries end up coming up and of course I believe in boundaries. I also believe of giving a lot of yourself and giving back within reflective supervision. But one of the questions that I asked today with somebody who was talking about a family that they ended up spending a lot of time with was, 'how much did the immigrations status lead to this amount of time?' and it was multiple hours. This family had complex needs because of their refugee status and I think it was this but also because of what it brought up in the provider. The provider's strong need to offer services to a group of individuals who were not getting the services that they needed.

If I had one thing to add, and I think I would say this about anybody that works with young children, and specifically in thinking about the refugee population, I do really think about reflective consultation or providing care for the providers. Both inform critical self-reflection, like what are we not seeing? What are we taking for granted? Being careful of that saviorism urge that I think brought many of us in the field. Then we have to sort of back-track and watch which I think we can and also just recognizing – being able to give off yourself, so being able to get back. I just think that the holding of the holders is so important.

Unique contexts, global principles

Our two participants, one a primary grade teacher from Northern Ireland and the other a psychologist from the United States, offered interesting perspectives on the importance of self-care for individuals who support families with refugee backgrounds. Our teacher has a leadership role in welcoming newly arrived families in a school that has become a revolving door for refugee resettlement. He is regularly exposed to horrific stories of loss and he spends much time supporting individuals trying to move ahead and create new lives in an unfamiliar place. He understands that such exposure takes a toll on his well-being and meets monthly with a psychologist to help process the trauma. He is clear this counselling is beneficial. The American educational psychologist we interviewed was extremely concerned about the confidentiality of her clients. She stressed the need for educators to set up boundaries for their own well-being, but quickly acknowledged caring individuals who work with refugee families often ignore their own boundaries. Her observation that educators take it upon themselves to do more, to give more to families in need, is both true and cautionary. She warns that educators can act on a 'saviourism' urge that can have negative effects for all involved. Most notably, the value she ascribes to counselling is twofold. Firstly, the sessions offer care for educators and, secondly, the sessions offer an opportunity to critically reflect on and improve practice.

Individuals who find themselves supporting young children and families with refugee backgrounds are fated to learn details about atrocities, suffering, and loss. Across our years of research, participants have offered multiple accounts of young children innocently sharing horrifying stories with their peers and parents confiding tragic events to their children's teachers. For some of society's most compassionate individuals, those drawn to caring for young children, learning of these experiences most certainly takes a toll. And, as the psychologist we interviewed offered, carers often invest more of themselves when families have greatly suffered. Staff in preschools, childcare centres, and playgroups that serve families with refugee backgrounds should have opportunities to meet with mental health workers to discuss what they are experiencing. These conversations offer both opportunities to address the effects of vicarious trauma and also a chance for critical reflection about how carers engage in their work.

Conclusion

Wars, famine, and resulting forced migration are ugly things that inflict trauma on their victims and on those who work to care for the victims. For educators and others who support young children with refugee backgrounds, working to understand the many ways trauma can manifest itself is challenging but important. Trauma can delay emotional development, lead to health issues and inappropriate behaviours, and hinder academic growth. Yet, the impacts of trauma can be inconsistent and young children who are often resilient can demonstrate surprising improvements. For individuals who work with these children and families, it is imperative they set boundaries, seek regular support, and tend to their own well-being or else they risk losing their ability to make a difference.

References

Alayarian, A. (2018). *Handbook of working with children, trauma, and resilience: An intercultural psychoanalytic view.* Taylor & Francis Group.

Arar, K., Brooks, J., & Bogotch, I. (2019). *Education, immigration and migration policy, leadership and praxis for a changing world.* Emerald Publishing.

Arar, K., Orucu, D., & Kucukcayir, G. (2018). These students need love and affection: Experience of a female school leader with the challenges of Syrian refugee education. *Leading and Managing, 24*(2), 28–43.

Aviles, A. M., Anderson, T. R., & Davila, E. R. (2006). Child and adolescent social–emotional development within the context of school. *Child and Adolescent Mental Health, 11*(1), 32–39. https://doi.org/10.1111/j.1475-3588.2005.00365.x

Barowsky, E. I., & McIntyre, T. (2010). Migration and relocation trauma of young refugees and asylum seekers: Awareness as prelude to effective intervention. *Childhood Education, 86*(3), 161–168.

Betancourt, T. S., Newnham, E. A., Layne, C. M., Kim, S., Steinberg, A. M., Ellis, H., & Birman, D. (2012). Trauma history and psychopathology in war-affected refugee children referred for trauma-related mental health services in the United States. *Journal of Traumatic Stress, 25*(6), 682–690.

Blodgett, C., & Lanigan, J. D. (2018). The association between adverse childhood experience (ACE) and school success in elementary school children. *School Psychology Quarterly, 33*(1), 137. https://doi.org/10.1037/spq0000256

Branson, D. C. (2019). Vicarious trauma, themes in research, and terminology: A review of literature. *Traumatology, 25,* 2–10. https://doi.org/10.1037/trm0000161

Briere, J., Johnson, K., Bissada, A., Damon, L., Crouch, J., Gil, E., Hanson, R., & Ernst, V. (2001). The trauma symptom checklist for young children (TSCYC): Reliability and association with abuse exposure in a multi-site study. *Child Abuse & Neglect, 25*(8), 1001–1014. https://doi.org/10.1016/S0145-2134(01)00253-8

Cameron, C. D., Hutcherson, C. A., Ferguson, A. M., Scheffer, J. A., Hadjiandreou, E., & Inzlicht, M. (2019). Empathy is hard work: People choose to avoid empathy because of its cognitive costs. *Journal of experimental psychology: General, 148*(6), 962–976. https://doi.org/10.1037/xge0000595

Chen, E., Cohen, S., & Miller, G. E. (2009). How low socioeconomic status affects 2-year hormonal trajectories in children. *Psychological Science, 21*(1), 31–37. https://doi.org/10.1177/0956797609355566

Coulter, S., & Mooney, S. (2018). Much more than PTSD: Mothers' narratives of the impact of trauma on child survivors and their families. *Contemporary Family Therapy, 40*(3), 226–236. https://doi.org/10.1007/s10591-017-9408-z

Davidson, N., Skull, S., Burgner, D., Kelly, P., Raman, S., Silove, D., Steel, Z., Vora, R., & Smith, M. (2004). An issue of access: Delivering equitable health care for newly arrived refugee children in Australia. *Journal of Paediatrics and Child Health, 40*(9–10), 569–575.

Davidson, N., Skull, S., Chaney, G., Frydenberg, A., Isaacs, D., Kelly, P., Lampropoulos, B., Raman, S., Silove, D., & Buttery, J. (2004). Comprehensive health assessment for newly arrived refugee children in Australia. *Journal of Paediatrics and Child Health, 40*(9–10), 562–568.

De Bellis, M. (2005). The psychobiology of neglect. *Child Maltreatment, 10*(2), 150–172.

Dryden-Peterson, S. (2017). Refugee education: Education for an unknowable future. *Curriculum Inquiry, 47*(1), 14–24. https://doi.org/10.1080/03626784.2016.1 255935

Edgeworth, K. (2013). *Refugees in rural schools: Issues of space, racism and (un)belonging.* Australian Association for Research in Education Conference, Adelaide, South Australia.

Fazel, M., & Stein, A. (2002). The mental health of refugee children. *Archives of Disease in Childhood, 87*(5), 366–370.

Felitti, V. J., Anda, R. F., Nordenberg, D., Williamson, D. F., Spitz, A. M., Edwards, V., Koss, M. P., & Marks, J. S. (1998). Relationship of childhood abuse and household dysfunction to many of the leading causes of death in adults. *American Journal of Preventive Medicine, 14*(4), 245–258. https://doi.org/10.1016/s0749-3797(98)00017-8

Fraser, J. G., Noroña, C. R., Bartlett, J. D., Zhang, J., Spinazzola, J., Griffin, J. L., Montagna, C., Todd, M., Bodian, R., & Barto, B. (2019). Screening for trauma symptoms in child welfare-involved young children: Findings from a statewide trauma-informed care initiative. *Journal of Child & Adolescent Trauma, 12*(3), 399–409. https://doi.org/10.1007/s40653-018-0240-x

Frater-Mathieson, K. (2004). Refugee trauma, loss and grief: Implications for intervention. In R. Hamilton & D. Moore (Eds.), *Educational Interventions for Refugee Children* (pp. 12–34). Routledge.

Gao, Y., Borlam, D., & Zhang, W. (2015). The association between heart rate reactivity and fluid intelligence in children. *Biological Psychology, 107*, 69–75. https://doi.org/10.1016/j.biopsycho.2015.03.006

Hart, R. (2009). Child refugees, trauma and education: Interactionist considerations on social and emotional needs and development. *Educational Psychology in Practice, 25*(4), 351–368. https://doi.org/10.1080/02667360903315172

Kim, J., Chesworth, B., Franchino-Olsen, H., & Macy, R. J. (2022). A scoping review of vicarious trauma interventions for service providers working with people who have experienced traumatic events. *Trauma Violence Abuse, 23*(5), 1437–1460. https://doi.org/10.1177/1524838021991310

Lorek, A., Ehntholt, K., Nesbitt, A., Wey, E., Githinji, C., Rossor, E., & Wickramasinghe, R. (2009). The mental and physical health difficulties of children held within a British immigration detention center: A pilot study. *Child Abuse & Neglect, 33*(9), 573–585.

Mace, A. O., Mulheron, S., Jones, C., & Cherian, S. (2014). Educational, developmental and psychological outcomes of resettled refugee children in Western Australia: A review of school of special educational needs: medical and mental health input. *Journal of Paediatrics and Child Health, 50*(12), 985–992. https://doi.org/10.1111/jpc.12674

Mares, S., & Jureidini, J. (2004). Psychiatric assessment of children and families in immigration detention: Clinical, administrative and ethical issues. *Australian and New Zealand Journal of Public Health, 28*(6), 520–526.

Marriage, S., & Marriage, K. (2005). Too many sad stories: Clinician stress and coping. *The Canadian Child and Adolescent Psychiatry Review, 14*(4), 114–117.

McCann, L., & Pearlman, L. (1990). Vicarious traumatization a framework for understanding psychological effects of working with victims. *Journal of Traumatic Stress., 3*(1), 131–149.

McDonald, M. K., Borntrager, C. F., & Rostad, W. (2014). Measuring trauma: Considerations for assessing complex and non-PTSD criterion a childhood trauma. *Journal of Trauma & Dissociation*, 15(2), 184–203. https://doi.org/10.1080/15299 732.2014.867577

McLean, S. (2016). The effect of trauma on the brain development of children. http://newcastle.summon.serialssolutions.com/2.0.0/link/0/eLvHCXMwrV1LS 8QwEB5cPSheFBWfkPtS7TNtDx7EB6Iuiq54DGmagEJb2F3x7ztJm3a7B0F2L6 GENvmamZbJ5JsZgMA_d52FfwKPQu4GucDNRxxEVAo09F3BI-nFgaAyNeRC-jBKPm78cVOQdGroXvSrSH5yf_aX5C-WFj32ofB1KO0_xN8Oih14jUqALaoBtg-sWcs8Xq70mfMKHI_EkrQZ0mlHTOAxBYMK_C96cGQwzXTHCRlJZnoAN-J73EHiLHgKTI9nW0WjCTtDAb30p3Y7S0wQZ6qZ1KY9-cuqrl-d-Z9WURGgfi-grOqpIhWGbAsjmwrFLMgmU0iuKA6QF1evMi_xSzS1k6728DGMSp3jt3QJqsX-O0cvUQHxgYY78C2jgshOmADse3Cmiz3IMXFJPVikkqRejFJVRLERww-Mod-P32Lx7cPr3e34-t7REzGTtFJO2XJv6h7AelmV8hAIVaGveMKVSGSoqMiy3FN-JlgnJvTBX6ggeVzjx8UpHO4GtTsFOYUPhNyLPYNMUu9G0hF8YzUve

Montgomery, E. (2010). Trauma and resilience in young refugees: A 9-year follow-up study. *Development and Psychopathology*, 22(2), 477–489. https://doi.org/10.1017/ S0954579410000180

Moran, R. J., & Asquith, N. L. (2020). Understanding the vicarious trauma and emotional labour of criminological research. *Methodological Innovations*, 13(2), 205979912092608. https://doi.org/10.1177/2059799120926085

Oberg, C. (2019). The Arc of Migration and the Impact on Children's Health and Well-Being: Forward to the Special Issue-Children on the Move. *Children (Basel)*, 6(9), 100.

Payne, R. (2001). *A framework for understanding poverty*. Aha Process Inc.

Pross, C. (2006). Trauma, vicarious traumatization and its prevention. *Trauma*, 16(1), 1–66.

Ratcliffe, M. (2012). Phenomenology as a form of empathy. *Inquiry*, 55(5), 473–495. https://doi.org/10.1080/0020174x.2012.716196

Romano, E., Babchishin, L., Marquis, R., & Fréchette, S. (2015). Childhood maltreatment and educational outcomes. *Trauma, Violence, & Abuse*, 16(4), 418–437.

Sapmaz, Ş. Y., Tanrıverdi, B. U., Öztürk, M., Gözaçanlar, Ö., Ülker, G. Y., & Özkan, Y. (2017). Immigration-related mental health disorders in refugees 5–18 years old living in Turkey. *Neuropsychiatric Disease and Treatment*, 13, 2813–2821.

Scheeringa, M. S., & Zeanah, C. H. (2001). A relational perspective on PTSD in early childhood. *Journal of Traumatic Stress*, 14(4), 799–815. https://doi. org/10.1023/a:1013002507972

Schore, A. N. (2015). Plenary address, Australian childhood foundation conference childhood trauma: Understanding the basis of change and recovery early right brain regulation and the relational origins of emotional wellbeing. *Children Australia*, 40(2), 104–113. https://doi.org/10.1017/cha.2015.13

Sellars, M. (2010). *Intrapersonal intelligence, executive function and stage three students*. Australian Catholic University.

Sellars, M., Imig, S., & Fischetti, J. (2022). *Creating spaces of wellbeing and belonging for refugee and asylum-seeker students; Skills and strategies for classroom teachers*. Routledge.

Steimel, S. (2016). Negotiating refugee empowerment(s) in resettlement organizations. *Journal of Immigrant & Refugee Studies*, 15(1), 90–107. https://doi.org/ 10.1080/15562948.2016.1180470

Stewart, E., & Mulvey, G. (2013). Seeking safety beyond refuge: The impact of immigration and citizenship policy upon refugees in the UK. *Journal of Ethnic and Migration Studies, 40*(7), 1023–1039. https://doi.org/10.1080/13691 83x.2013.836960

Stolbach, B. C., Minshew, R., Rompala, V., Dominguez, R. Z., Gazibara, T., & Finke, R. (2013). Complex trauma exposure and symptoms in urban traumatized children: A preliminary test of proposed criteria for developmental trauma disorder. *Journal of Traumatic Stress, 26*(4), 483–491. https://doi.org/10.1002/jts.21826

Sutton, L., Rowe, S., Hammerton, G., & Billings, J. (2022). The contribution of organisational factors to vicarious trauma in mental health professionals: A systematic review and narrative synthesis. *European Journal of Psychotraumatology, 13*(1). https://doi.org/10.1080/20008198.2021.2022278

Teicher, M. H., Andersen, S. L., Polcari, A., Anderson, C. M., Navalta, C. P., & Kim, D. M. (2003). The neurobiological consequences of early stress and childhood maltreatment. *Neuroscience & Biobehavioral Reviews, 27*(1–2), 33–44.

Theisen-Womersley, G. (2021). *Trauma and resilience among displaced populations.* https://doi.org/10.1007/978-3-030-67712-1

Twardosz, S., & Lutzker, J. R. (2010). Child maltreatment and the developing brain: A review of neuroscience perspectives. *Aggression and Violent Behavior, 15*(1), 59–68.

Vervliet, M., Meyer Demott, M. A., Jakobsen, M., Broekaert, E., Heir, T., & Derluyn, I. (2014). The mental health of unaccompanied refugee minors on arrival in the host country. *Scandinavian Journal of Psychology, 55*(1), 33–37. https://doi.org/10.1111/sjop.12094

Weiland, C., Barata, M. C., & Yoshikawa, H. (2014). The co-occurring development of executive function skills and receptive vocabulary in preschool-aged children: A look at the direction of the developmental pathways. *Infant and Child Development, 23*(1), 4–21. https://doi.org/10.1002/icd.1829

Weiss, S. J. (2007). Neurobiological alterations associated with traumatic stress. *Perspectives in Psychiatric Care, 43*(3), 114–122. https://doi.org/10.1111/j.1744-6163.2007.00120.x

Womersley, G. T. (2021). *Trauma and resilience among displaced populations: A sociocultural exploration.* Springer.

Yang, W., Roig, M., Jimenez, M., Perry, J., & Shepherd, A. (2016). *Leaving no one behind: The imperative of inclusive development.*

Ziegler, D. (2011). *Traumatic experience and the brain* (2nd ed.). Acacia Pub Inc.

Chapter 3

The critical nature of inclusion, its principles, and parameters

Introduction

Arriving in a new country after suffering great loss is an overwhelming proposition. Now, imagine coupling that with the imperative to learn a new language, comprehend a new culture, enter a new education system, and meet the demands of your new host country or resettlement service. For people with refugee backgrounds who are on this journey, there are numerous touch points where systems, institutions, and individuals can improve or confound the experience. This chapter offers research on the ways policies, places, and people support newly arrived children and their families and offers insights from individuals working to create inclusive organisations in multiple countries.

Systemic inclusion

The term 'authentic inclusion' presents multiple challenges and ethical issues for educators and carers of the young. These challenges can be determined at all three levels of the structures into which babies, toddlers, and young children are cared for and educated outside the home, prompting the question of inclusion into what exactly? What may be considered authentic about the inclusive policies and strategies that are formulated and actioned by those entrusted with the care and education of these babies, toddlers, and young children? The notion of inclusion is not automatic sensation. It is not simply reliant on an invitation or a request to participate in an event or activity. Critically, the sense of being included is heavily reliant on participants, including the very young, having a sense of belonging (Sellars, 2021a, 2021b; Sellars & Murphy, 2017; Shuker & Cherrington, 2016). Goodenow and Grady (1993, p. 80) define belonging as a feelings of being 'accepted, respected, included and supported by others,' while Sellars (2020, p. 88) identified it as 'encompassing feelings of connectedness and positivity.' In the context of the traumas that have invariably impacted on the lives of young refugee and asylum-seeker communities, developing these emotional capacities may present considerable challenges and are heavily reliant on the development of positive, authentically

DOI: 10.4324/9781003404231-4

supportive relationships (Sellars, 2020). Additionally, school belonging may be experienced differently by individuals of different cultural backgrounds (Chiu et al., 2016) and varying socio-economic backgrounds and experiences, which not only adds complexity to the question of inclusion but to the development of policies and practices at the systemic level. For many, the 'culture' of the caring and educational environments in which babies, toddlers, and young children are placed is a strong determinant of the degree to which these children are able to develop the sense of belonging that evidences authentic inclusion.

At the systemic level, to accommodate extremely diverse groups of children, such as those with refugee and asylum-seeker experiences, the policies and practices that are designed to facilitate inclusion must be well informed, strategically formulated, and available for sensitive implementation. To understand the complexity of the development of such policies, it may be important to consider the relationship between culture and ethos. Culture and ethos appear to have different characteristics (Glover & Coleman, 2005; McLaughlin, 2005). Discussing school ethos, Solvason (2005) determined ethos was a product of the culture, arguing that culture was more tangible and that ethos was a nebulous term in the context of educational research. This perspective was supported by Glover and Coleman (2005, 257), who, in their investigation of the interchangeability of the terms school culture, school ethos, and school climate, determined that school ethos was a term that was less easily measured, more 'subjective' in nature, and was more 'general' than the other terms under discussion. More importantly, however, is the distinction made by Donnelly (2000) between the formal, documented aspects of ethos and the lived reality of this expression in the real contexts of learning environments. As noted by Eisner (in Mc Laughlin, 2005), there frequently exists an important gap between these two categories of ethos. As both the formal and the experiential notions of ethos are heavily values laden, this lack of congruence between the two can present additional difficulties for children with refugee experiences, accentuating the various interpretations of the core values and foundational rationales under which these learning and caring environments operate and obscuring pathways to authentic belonging and inhibiting the degree to which authentic inclusion is possible.

While policymakers may espouse the aspirational aspects of their aims and outcomes statements and organisational ethos, it is the commitment to the values espoused by these documented guidelines that has the potential to provide opportunities, experiences, and resources that facilitate inclusion. Critical examination of policies at all levels of childcare, preschool, and school systems need to be interrogated systematically to reveal the values inherent in the documents. They must reflect a sincere acknowledgement and acceptance of the intrinsic worth of diversity and difference so that authentic inclusive practices may be successfully planned and executed. To ignore these values is not only ethically irresponsible, but also has the potential to promote assimilation. The psychological and social dangers of assimilation are well documented (see, for example, Berry, 2009; Berry et al., 2006; Betancourt et al., 2012; Correa-Velez et al., 2010; Doná & Berry, 1994; Ellis et al., 2008; Goodnow, 2014; Isik-Ercan et al., 2016). This is because assimilation requires all newcomers to adopt all the characteristics of their new cultural context, negating and neglecting their initial cultural heritage, traditions, language, and antecedents. Conversely, strategies which are based on integration, as opposed to assimilation, allow for the promotion of more authentic inclusion of the developmental and learning needs of these babies, toddlers, and young children and are aimed at respecting and dignifying the core aspects of heritage and first culture. Central to achieving this successfully for cohorts with widely diverse backgrounds, experiences, and influences is a sincere appreciation of the first language, cultural mores, religious affiliations, and other aspects of the societies and homes into which these babies, children, and toddlers return at the end of the day. The tightrope walked by policymakers and practitioners alike is how to make these considerations valuable, genuine aspects of the educational and caring environments that are provided for these children in the contexts of their new homelands, which are invariably dominated by 'white' 'western,' and 'middle class' beliefs and ways of doing and knowing.

Research findings

One of the key realisations gained by interviewing participants in multiple countries is how much local and national context matter in the ways refugees are treated. A teacher in Northern Ireland and a playgroup provider in New Zealand illustrate the disparate ways refugees can be perceived and integrated in different parts of the world.

> *Context:* I coordinate multiple multicultural playgroups in New Zealand which are free of charge and open to everyone. But particularly the refugee and migrant communities. We have like 500 playgroups around New Zealand, and they are early childhood education. The parents come too, it's not a drop-off service. The parents run the play centre and run every aspect. I do come from a teaching background. I was a primary school teacher.
>
> The other thing I think is really important is the place of our Māori within our playgroup. New Zealand is a bicultural country, and so that's vitally important. I think if nothing else, they understand the value and the importance we place on multicultural in this country. It's not just something nice to have, it's at the centre. But I think culturally, it might be closer to their own cultures. You know that value of family, that value of the extended family. You know, value that placed on relationships and hospitality, you know. So, it's a sense of belonging to the place.

When I started this job, I thought there would be more separation between the different cultures or religions, but it hasn't been. It's been quite amazing how that has never come up as an issue. So, one thing we do is a lot of celebrating of festivals. I think that's so important, a big deal in these cultures. We are doing them together in the playgroup. It's really beautiful to see, you know we had a big party just the other day. It was Persian New Year. It's a big deal for Afghani people. It's the biggest day we did, and we did the traditional way it's done. You know, all of those other festivals that we have. We've got Eid coming up. You know we got that holy holiday Easter. The only rule is that you have to be okay with everyone's religious faith. The other way we manage it is we make it pretty secular. So, when you're celebrating Eid, no one is saying a prayer or anything that would probably make the Hindu moms feel uncomfortable. Then you know, it's okay to join in. But I think it's important that you see yourself reflected in what we're doing at the playgroup.

Context: Our school is almost 40% from a refugee or asylum background. A lot of our families are housed in hotels and some of the hotels are nearby to the school. We have a reputation basically of being a school where, if you speak English as a second language, you know, you might want to send your children there, so that kind of attracts them as well. But, until you actually live here, you don't really understand it. Given our history [Catholic and Protestant conflict known as the *Troubles*], it's a bit of a siege mentality for some communities. You know, where they feel like they're surrounded by enemies and then, when they find other people come in, and it's like more enemies coming in, you know that mentality of defending what we've got.

I'm saying the policy in the UK has become extremely harsh, extremely punitive. It's become very, very harsh and performative. Really, [politicians] are getting votes from people by stigmatizing these families, and, you know, we've got over a 100, nearly 200,000 Ukrainian refugees in in the UK. Nobody's bothered about that. Nobody batted an eye about that. But they can't seem to find, you know, 50 under 50,000 people, they can't absorb those people into society, you know whether it's seeming like a major problem. Now to me, if we had a well-functioning society, we would be able absorb these people no problem, you know. If our health service, if our housing was right, these people would be able to come in and work and have a normal life like we've allowed the Ukrainians to do by and large. So, it's very difficult time in the UK, working in this sector, working with these people. It's very hard at the moment, even harder for them. Obviously. So, it's not a great time really for refugees in the UK. It's very sad, because it's always been difficult, but you know there was a lot of good stuff going on, a lot of good will. There is a lot of good will still, but that doesn't seem to come through to the political sphere at all at the moment, and even the opposition parties aren't really opposing it as you hoped they would.

Unique contexts, global principles

There is an adage in educational research that the variance in practice within a school is often much greater than the variance between any two schools. Likely it is fair to apply this same adage to countries and the ways newly arrived refugees are treated. Our New Zealand playgroup leader highlighted the way her country has come to value its Māori peoples and their commitment to extended family, relationships, and hospitality. She believes this has created a welcoming environment for families with refugee backgrounds as many share the same strong emphasis on family and relationships. She also asserts New Zealand is a society respectful of diverse faiths and she has crafted a playgroup environment that allows individuals to share and engage around religion in a non-threatening manner. Her experience is contrasted with our teacher from Northern Ireland who finds himself working in a broader society he believes is unwelcoming to newly arrived families, specifically families from places like Afghanistan, Syria, and African nations. He is cognisant of the fact that his community has a history of violence based on religious differences and national identity. He also points to the blanket acceptance of 200,000 Ukrainian refugees as a sign other concerning issues are at play. This teacher is angry that welcoming and supporting people forcibly displaced from their homes has become a political issue no party wants to touch. Yet, despite this broader reality, he has worked closely with his colleagues to create a space where young students and their parents with refugee backgrounds feel welcome.

With some jobs, it is possible to close your door, focus on the work, and shut out what is happening at a systemic level. Working with young children and families with refugee backgrounds is not one of those jobs. When these vulnerable families struggle to find dignity, face overt and subtle racism, and come up against systems that make them feel unwelcome, it has negative effects on their well-being. When parents are depressed, anxious, and hopeless, there are often ripple effects for young children. For educators, this brings additional challenges into the classroom and puts added pressure on them. Our research participant from Northern Ireland works extra hard to create an island of safety and belonging in his school for families with refugee backgrounds to counteract the caustic policies he sees at play in his community. Conversely, our New Zealand participant is confident she is part of a broader system with the best interests of refugees in mind. In her case, she can leverage services and supports to further assist her students. Foundational to meeting the needs of vulnerable families is knowledge and this includes a knowledge of national- and state-level refugee and asylum-seeker policies, practices, and systems. Understanding the unique challenges your families are facing offers insights and information that can be used to guide practice.

Institutional inclusion

Institutional sensitivity is critical to the ways in which their own policies and other mandatory documentation, developed under the guidelines of the systemic bodies, allow for authentic inclusion. At the level of the childcare centre, the preschool, and the school itself, inclusion, even for the youngest child, does not occur randomly or even serendipitously in many cases. Inclusion needs to be planned, needs to involve all the carers and educators, and needs to blend the diverse aspects of the home culture and that of the new homeland as seamlessly as possible (Sellars, 2021a, 2021b). Many young children, most especially those with backgrounds of displacement and trauma, need to hear familiar language, eat food with which they are accustomed, and follow routines with which they are comfortable. While this may require alterations to routines and generally organised guidelines, on closer inspection, many of these may have no solid theoretical foundations, instead being created by organisational or perceived efficiency considerations. Caring and learning environments that espouse inclusion need to be flexible, open to alternatives, and creative in their problem-solving approaches.

One such example was provided by a primary school principal. The school lunchtime routine and supervision did not support the customary mealtime practices of one refugee family of several sisters newly enrolled in the school. Their meal was brought by eldest sister to be shared and served by her to her siblings. The usual routine of students sitting in their class groups to be supervised by their own teachers did not allow for this to happen, with teachers of the younger students being concerned that they did not have any lunch. The sisters had to find a quiet place on the playground to eat after the other students had gone to play, limiting their interaction with the other students and isolating themselves as 'different.' Lacking any solid rationale for the lunchtime routine to be organised in that way, the principal simply organised the school differently, facilitating the traditional meal sharing, maximising their opportunities to be included during the official eating time and in the socialising activities later. Conversely, observations of the experience of a preschooler in a less formal institution were not so pleasant. She was unable to eat the food supplied as she was unfamiliar with the taste and smell. The centre policy did not permit parents to bring food from home for their children, so the child in question remained distressed and hungry every day. Similarly, a childcare centre ruled that each toddler was allowed to bring only one item from home to comfort them, irrespective of the child's emotional needs. The former incident, while in a very formal systemic institution, evidenced a deep understanding of the complexity of inclusion. The less formal contexts, which were provided for younger students, displayed an indifference for the needs of individual children, irrespective of the values in their mission statements. Building the sense of belonging necessitates children to feel nurtured and cared for, despite their diverse needs, and is a cornerstone of authentic inclusion.

The most prominent theme in discussions of strategies to promote belonging and inclusion revolves around connecting the child's heritage and their experiences in their new homeland. This may require planning activities that are specifically designed to promote multicultural, multilingual caring and teaching and learning environments. One of the dominant factors in successful resettlement and societal inclusion is the role of language. Language competencies are recognised as a critical aspect of any integration programme (Dooley & Thangaperumal, 2011; Wofford & Tibi, 2018). However, this term is usually interpreted as language that is used by the dominant groups in society, with little reference to the importance of the role of first language to children's capacities to become included as members of the two societies, two cultures, and the numerous communities that comprise their multiple worlds. Many of the babies, toddlers, and young children who participate in childcare centres, preschools, and the early years of schooling are only exposed to the language of the majority societal group once they are outside of their own homes. Although learning the language of new homelands is a necessary and beneficial aspect of inclusion as members of society in their new homelands (Emert, 2014; Hek, 2005; Watters, 2007; Wofford & Tibi, 2018), incorporating first language experiences into the caring and educational contexts they experience as babies, toddlers, and young children may contribute significantly to children's sense of belonging and inclusion (Sellars, 2020, 2021a, 2021b; Sellars et al., 2023). Strategies were employed by carers and educators of these young refugees to develop positive, caring, and safe relationships, including basic phrases in the first language of their children and using these as greetings and informal conversation. They routinely ensure the provision of culturally familiar, appropriate foods, engage them in games, books, playthings, storytelling, songs, and other media which are reflective of the students' respective cultural heritages and cultures in ways that are respectful and can be shared by the entire community.

Research findings

Nearly every participant in our research focused on the need for their own organisation to continually adapt to support newly arrived families. We spoke with a Government school consultant in England and a centre director in Australia who offered insights about the programmes and practices they have implemented to foster inclusion.

> *Context:* I sit in the improvement team and we support schools in our county to make sure they've got the best provisions around a multitude of things, including English as an additional language, anti-racism, and of course, support for refugee and asylum seeking pupils. And obviously we've got areas that are extremely rural and mining communities. There is quite a lot of economic deprivation. We've seen a large number of families arriving

from Hong Kong and of course we've had Ukrainian refugees arriving as well. So they have been a significant change in the county's make up.

And what we did is we had a massive display in our entrance of the map of the world, with all of our young interpreters with the speech bubble saying hello in their home language and a little bit of information about the young interpreters. As soon as you walk in, you know that we have lots of languages for home languages. We were celebrating it. That meant that teachers knew what they were doing and gave that subtle message that this is fine. We have lots of languages, different home languages. We support pupils in acquiring their English at the same time as learning the curriculum. So I think those kinds of key messages that we gave to families put them at ease. We did language days as well. We had a Polish day. We had an Arabic day, and families came in, cooked for us; and we had activities where everybody joined in, and the children also learned little bits about those languages and cultures.

Context: I'm the director of a centre run by children's services, in the Australian migrant program [for newly arrived refugees]. The staff that we have here is incredible. All of our families we know have come from conflict or fleeing a terrible situation. We have an educator with training who herself was a refugee, and she's just incredible with knowing how to approach families and talk, but also with the reassuring. You know what we do. We are safe, and our main goal is to ensure that you would say you are comfortable. Because we know that learning will not occur until you are socially and emotionally ready.

The main advice with all early learning centres is to be extremely welcoming, giving a sense of belonging wherever you can. You know language is not just about words. It's about how you are with your body and your face and respect what they hope to get out of coming here. So, what I found works well is, and I'll also get to it in a moment, our educators are giving families the time they need to come in and be with their child throughout the day to see what we do.

Having aspects of their culture displayed in the room. Also, give them time. What we've found with many of our families is they are almost pressured into starting English classes or early learning far before they're ready because they feel like it's a part of their visa. This is what they get from the Settlement Service. Sometimes a bit of pressure is put on them to start straight away. We've found that attendance is extremely low in these cases because families simply aren't ready. So, we can offer half days, as I said, spending lots of time with their child, so they get a feel of connection with us as well. It's very important that they trust us to begin with. They see what we're doing will benefit their child and give them the first freedom they've probably had in a long time. So, getting to that point can be difficult sometimes. But we get that.

Unique contexts, global principles

Developing inclusive organisations requires staff to continuously focus on creating opportunities to help young children feel valued. In the case of our English consultant, she offered strategies at play in her schools. The school entrance display of languages from around the world enabled families to feel both welcome and part of a very diverse community. Hosting days based on home countries, and having the families provide their native foods and discuss their cultures, sent message that different cultures are valued. While the strategies helped families feel valued, this participant also asserted such practices foster shared beliefs among the staff. Our Australian director keeps safety and comfort at the core of her centre vision. The centre she runs serves young children while their parents engage in English instruction on the same premises. Acknowledging most of her families have fled their homelands and have experienced trauma, she talked of the importance of caring words and purposeful body language. She also focused on respecting the needs and wants of her students' parents by offering opportunities for them to attend shortened days, enabling them to have more time with their young children. In both cases, our participants displayed a concern for acknowledging their families as unique individuals.

Being forcibly displaced means you lose all sense of personal agency. From living in refugee camps to arriving in new homelands, families are at the mercy of the organisations and individuals tasked with their resettlement. While our Australian participant noted the local resettlement agency was pushing families to conform quickly, she offered families autonomy to control their schedule. By respecting the needs of parents and young children, schools, day care centres, and playgroups can help to rebuild confidence and self-worth. Carers need to remain vigilant that parents who may have lost everything and lived through hell may need to be with their own children until they are comfortable being apart. Building trust and fostering integration is an iterative process: purposefully making little and big efforts, changing attendance policies and putting up welcome signs, holding country days and inviting families to share their home culture, smiling towards the newly arrived mother and her young daughter. These practices in isolation make individuals feel welcome. But, in concert, these practices promote a caring staff and develop an inclusive organisation.

Individual inclusion

Irrespective of the policies and procedure which govern the institutions in which refugee babies, toddlers, and young children are cared for and educated, the ways in which these are interpreted, planned, and actioned are the result of individuals, either alone or in groups. Working with diverse groups in any community is not simply a matter of learning how to work effectively with interpreters, being aware of the national characteristics such as food, festivals, traditional dress, flags, and other outward indicators of nationality. It requires a deeper understanding of ways in which individuals were culturally socialised and flexibility to solve differences appropriately (Sellars et al., 2023). The impact of one individual's creativity may support others in their awareness of authentic inclusion, just as the misguided strategies of another result in developing the characteristics of assimilation. Leaders in the centres and schools who support these young refugees and asylum seekers may take much of the responsibility for initiatives that foster belonging and inclusion, but it is individuals who realise these in action. Directors of early years centres and school leaders frequently seek out staff who are multilingual and speak at least one of the languages or dialects that is spoken by the children in their care. In one example, a school principal created a parent café (Bradley & Sellars, 2021). He also developed a plan of 'strategic staffing.' He sought out and employed qualified individuals whose ethnicity reflected the diversity of his refugee and asylum-seeker students. He invited local community members who had previously held refugee and asylum-seeker status to join the volunteers at the school and permitted his teachers to invite parents into their classrooms to become familiar with the routines of the school day and the pedagogical strategies used in the school. Although many of the parents had little or no English, they were encouraged to participate in a helping role rather than sit quietly and observe, allowing them to be included in the classroom management. Acknowledging the importance of parents and community in the care and education of children, while important for all children, may be critical for young children with refugee and asylum-seeker backgrounds who have experiences of loss and displacement.

It is equally important, however, that all the adults who are interacting with these young children are cognisant of the subtle ways in which inclusive practices are designed to be all encompassing, to meet the needs of all the babies, toddlers, and young children in various, differentiated ways, and to provide a comprehensive, broad perspective on what is necessary for these children to learn and develop positively. Inclusion requires that the essential needs, interests, and cultural demands of these early childhood cohorts are met within the wider landscape of all the children being cared for and educated in their contexts. The challenge to work with empathy and compassion (Nussbaum, 2001) without permitting these emotions to dominate the planning and actioning inclusive strategies not only supports the development of a sense of belonging for all children, but also avoids the emotional 'traps' that may otherwise lead to unintentional 'othering' (Foucault, 1991; Said, 1978) of the babies, toddlers, and young children with refugee and asylum-seeker backgrounds.

Research findings

The strength of any organisation is the quality of the people it employs. In caring organisations like preschools, day care centres, and playgroups, this is even more of a truism. We spoke with a manager who supports migrants and refugee families in Australia and a head teacher of a very diverse school in England who shared insights about the ways they instil an ethic of care in their staff members.

> *Context:* I'm, the executive head teacher at this primary school. I knew that I wanted to work in disadvantaged communities. That's something I knew. I knew that I wanted to make a difference for people that society kind of has stuff stacked up against. This is one of the most deprived of the core cities in England. So, a community that faces a huge number of challenges very diverse, which I also love. We got, you know, young people and families from all over the world.

> If we have this compelling vision if this is what we believe in. And if people contradict that, it's my job and the job of the leadership team and other people in school to say that's not okay. Is that all right? No, it's not okay to talk about our families like that. So, it's about creating a culture within the school and knowing what we believe in, and we call it Topper's way. There's a really clear way we do things around here, which is about being respectful. That's about not making judgments about people. It's about not undermining our community members.

> *Context:* I have been working with this organisation supporting families for more than 20 years. Our team has lots of expertise and knowledge about the needs of these families in the programs I manage. Most of our educators are bilingual or multilingual, and we are very selective when we employ our educators.

> I don't talk much about empathy because you can't really have empathy, because you've never been in a refugee country for ten years of your life, and you don't know what life is like living in, you know, a refugee camp and having all sort of here. Services are often very busy environments, very compliant with lots of policies. It may be hard to find time to allocate for families. But investing in those early conversations and finding out will prove beneficial for that sense of trust because many refugee families will have lots of issues with trust. They come from countries where trust is very little, especially in government and government officials.

Unique contexts, global principles

A remarkable character trait shared by individuals in our research was having a clear vision and commitment to serving populations in need. The head teacher in England whom we interviewed talked in glowing terms about her school's vision and she was adamant her colleagues needed to share and fully understand that vision. In fact, she took it upon herself to challenge educators and community members who questioned the school or the families it serves. She places respect at the heart of her work and is insistent her staff get to know each student and parent as individuals, rather than making broad judgements. The manager interviewed in Australia also spoke of getting to know her families as a way of developing trust. She recognises the work of educators is demanding but insists time must be allocated to gaining understandings about families. She believes in investing in conversations to gain insights and is adamant carers can't really empathise with refugees as the lived realities of people forcibly removed from their homes are so far beyond the lives of most carers.

Individual inclusion is built on a simple premise, that each person, regardless of their circumstances, is unique and valuable and should be treated as such. While the work of carers can be demanding and all consuming, time must be set aside to learn about the individuals organisations serve. Being purposeful in learning about newly arrived children and parents, asking thoughtful questions, and avoiding judgements lay the groundwork for inclusion. A caution voiced by Nussbaum (2001), however, is carers will naturally attempt to go beyond understanding and empathise, and they should not allow this empathy to cloud their judgement or practices. Among our participants, there was an ethic of care and unwavering adherence to their organisation's mission and the families they serve. So strongly did our participants believe in their work, some were willing to publicly challenge internal and external critics. Developing an organisation where caring staff buy into the mission requires staff to both understand the mission and have the skills to attain it. It is ultimately the responsibility of leaders to hire well and educate their teams, so they are true partners in the work of creating effective and inclusive organisations.

Conclusion

Being valued and connected to others are profound human needs. For refugees and asylum seekers who are attempting to integrate in a host country, the policies and practices in place at the systemic, institutional, and individual levels can determine whether children and families thrive or falter. While there are certainly places that get it right, carers need to be mindful that government or resettlement policies that strip self-determination from people and dictate their decisions will further their trauma. Broader systemic policies and practices are often beyond the control of those who provide care at the ground level, it is the ground level where human connection can most positively improve lives. Making efforts to know about the lived experiences of children, recognising the unique homelands of families, celebrating languages, faith, and food are all ways to develop inclusion at the individual and institutional levels.

References

Berry, J. W. (2009). A critique of critical acculturation. *International Journal of Intercultural Relations, 33*(5), 361–371. https://doi.org/10.1016/j.ijintrel.2009.06.003

Berry, J. W., Horenczyk, G., & Kwak, K. (2006). *Immigrant youth in cultural transition: Acculturation, identity, and adaptation across national contexts.* Lawrence Erlbaum Associates.

Betancourt, T. S., Newnham, E. A., Layne, C. M., Kim, S., Steinberg, A. M., Ellis, H., & Birman, D. (2012). Trauma history and psychopathology in war-affected refugee children referred for trauma-related mental health services in the United States. *Journal of Traumatic Stress, 25*(6), 682–690.

Bradley, M., & Sellars, M. (2021). Parent cafe reflections. In *Making a spectacle: Examining curriculum/pedagogy as recovery from political trauma* (pp. 183–189). Information Age Publishing.

Chiu, M., Chow, B., McBride, C., & Mol, S. (2016). Students' sense of belonging at school in 41 countries: Cross-cultural variability. *Journal of Cross-Cultural Psychology, 47*(2), 175–196.

Correa-Velez, I., Gifford, S. M., & Barnett, A. G. (2010). Longing to belong: Social inclusion and wellbeing among youth with refugee backgrounds in the first three years in Melbourne, Australia. *Social Science & Medicine, 71*(8), 1399–1408. https://doi.org/10.1016/j.socscimed.2010.07.018

Doná, G., & Berry, J. W. (1994). Acculturation attitudes and acculturative stress of Central American refugees. *International Journal of Psychology, 29*(1), 57–70.

Donnelly, C. (2000). In pursuit of school ethos. *British Journal of Educational Studies, 48*(2), 134–154. https://doi.org/10.1111/1467-8527.t01-1-00138

Dooley, K., & Thangaperumal, P. (2011). Pedagogy and participation: Literacy education for low literate refugee students of African origin in a Western school system. *Language and Education, 25*(5), 385–397.

Ellis, B. H., MacDonald, H. Z., Lincoln, A. K., & Cabral, H. J. (2008). Mental health of Somali adolescent refugees: The role of trauma, stress, and perceived discrimination. *Journal of Consulting and Clinical Psychology, 76*(2). https://doi.org/10.1037/0022-006X.76.2.184

Emert, T. (2014). "Hear a story, tell a story, teach a story": Digital narratives and refugee middle schoolers. *Voices from the Middle, 21*(4), 33–39.

Foucault, M. (1991). Governmentality 87–104. In B. Burchell, G. Gordon, & B. Miller (Eds.), *The Foucault effect: Studies in governmentality.* Chicago University Press.

Glover, D., & Coleman, M. (2005). School culture, climate and ethos: Interchangeable or distinctive concepts? *Journal of In-Service Education, 31*(2), 251–272.

Goodnow, J. J. (2014). Refugees, asylum seekers, displaced persons: Children in precarious positions. In G. B. Melton, A. Ben-Arieh, J. Cashmore, G. S. Goodman, & N. K. Worley (Eds.), *The SAGE handbook of child research* (pp. 339–360). SAGE Publications.

Goodenow, K., & Grady, C. (1993). The relationship of school belonging and friends' values to academic motivation among urban adolescent students. *The Journal of Experimental Education, 62*(1), 60–71.

Hek, R. (2005). The role of education in the settlement of young refugees in the UK: The experiences of young refugees. *Practice (Birmingham, England), 17*(3), 157–171. https://doi.org/10.1080/09503150500285115

Isik-Ercan, Z., Demir-Dagdas, T., Cakmakci, H., Cava-Tadik, Y., & Intepe-Tingir, S. (2016). Multidisciplinary perspectives towards the education of young low-income immigrant children. *Early Child Development and Care, 187*(9), 1413–1432. https://doi.org/10.1080/03004430.2016.1173037

McLaughlin, T. (2005). The educative importance of ethos. *British Journal of Educational Studies, 53*(3), 306–325. https://doi.org/10.1111/j.1467-8527.2005.00297.x

Nussbaum, M. (2001). *Upheavals of thought: The intelligence of emotions.* Cambridge University Press.

Said, E. (1978). Introduction. *Orientalism.* Vintage Books.

Sellars, M. (2020). *Educating students with refugee and asylum seeker experiences: A commitment to humanity.* Verlag Barbara Budrich.

Sellars, M. (2021a). Being and belonging: Developing inclusive ethos. *International Journal of Leadership in Education.* https://doi.org/10.1080/13603124.2021.1942994

Sellars, M. (2021b). Planning for belonging: Including refugee and asylum seeker students. *Journal of Refugee Studies, 35*(1), 576–594. https://doi.org/10.1093/jrs/feab073

Sellars, M., Imig, S., & Fischetti, J. (2023). *Creating spaces of wellbeing and belonging for refugee and asylum-seeker students: Skills and strategies for classroom teachers.* Routledge. https://doi.org/10.4324/9781003207900

Sellars, M., & Murphy, H. (2017). Becoming Australian: A review of Southern Sudanese students' educational experiences. *International Journal of Inclusive Education, 22*(5), 490–509. https://doi.org/10.1080/13603116.2017.1373308

Shuker, M. J., & Cherrington, S. (2016). Diversity in New Zealand early childhood education: Challenges and opportunities. *International Journal of Early Years Education, 24*(2), 172–187. https://doi.org/10.1080/09669760.2016.1155148

Solvason, C. (2005). Investigating specialist school ethos … or do you mean culture? *Educational Studies, 31*(1), 85–94. https://doi.org/10.1080/0305569042000310985

Watters, C. (2007). *Refugee children: Towards the next horizon* (1st ed.). Taylor & Francis.

Wofford, M. C., & Tibi, S. (2018). A human right to literacy education: Implications for serving Syrian refugee children. *International Journal of Speech Language Pathology, 20*(1), 182–190. https://doi.org/10.1080/17549507.2017.1397746

Chapter 4

Cultural understandings of childhood and early childhood education

Introduction

Understandings of childhood, childhood development, and the place of the child in society and under the law are far from fixed. Instead, they are strongly culturally bound, and observers have noted many different understandings and attitudes towards childhood, with implications for family and public policy engagement with children across cultures. These distinctions resonate with different ideas about how and on what pathway young children's development occurs, the degree to which they are to be understood as fully under the private dominion of the family versus being recognised as having some level of autonomy in the eyes of society and the law. These varied cultural understandings of childhood and early child development lead to different conceptions of appropriate parenting practice and to very different ideas about how children's development should be encouraged (e.g. through play or through early immersion into chores, and family responsibilities). This chapter explores the implications of these cultural frames for early childhood educators, who will find themselves in the uneasy position of having to navigate, interpret, and translate between newly arrived families and the expectations of their new host societies.

Childhood and the law

That notions of childhood need to be understood with a understanding of culture and society may be surprising to some educators in Western, English-speaking contexts who are accustomed to the particular view of childhood that is presented and perpetuated in policy, legislation, and common practices. The following passage from Skolnick (1975 p38), whilst almost half a century old, is particularly pertinent to the interrogation of childhood from diverse cultural and social perspectives. It introduces the ways in which the law and studies in child development theory have a dominating influence on how childhood is conceptualised and protected, albeit through rather independent pathways.

DOI: 10.4324/9781003404231-5

It also serves to illustrate how child protection laws dominate childcare and educational practices, both in the home and out of home contexts.

> The other major formal codification of concepts of childhood, apart from the law, is found in the literature of developmental psychology. Although there are many fundamental similarities between legal and psychological concepts of childhood, there is little direct influence of one field on the other. Rather, the resemblances may be attributed to the fact that both fields reflect the assumptions of the larger society. It is argued particularly by developmental psychologists and reform-minded policymakers, that public policies should be more directly based on scientific knowledge of child development…. There are, however, a number of difficulties with the assumption that social sciences contain guidelines for policymakers. … [R]ather than being obvious or given, the policy implications of much research, including that on children, is problematic. To begin at the simplest level, the kinds of problems studied by social scientists may bear little relevance to the issues involved in policy decisions. Bronfenbrenner, a developmental psychologist, has, for example, recently written of his inability to answer many of the questions he was asked in his capacity as an expert witness. The questions dealt with such matters as the effects of half-day versus full-day group care, age-desegregated classrooms, etc. Bronfenbrenner could not answer these questions because they concern the impact on children of the enduring environments in which they live or might live. Such issues have been relatively neglected by researchers in favor of laboratory studies: As Bronfenbrenner sums it up: '[M]uch of American developmental psychology is the science of the behavior of children in strange situations with strange adults.'

Bronfenbrenner's dilemma in answering questions that related to specific aspects of childcare and education may elicit responses from multiple disciplines today, it also serves to illustrate the 'one size fits all' nature of law-making which currently prevails and the dominance of the majority society in determining the definitions and parameters of both.

For many children with refugee and asylum-seeker experiences and their families, the understanding of childhood and the laws that govern interactions with these very junior members of society are alien to their customary understandings and even to the law in their countries of origin.

Trusting their children to strangers in strange environments presents potentially seismic challenges for newly arrived families. Out-of-home care may raise questions about child supervision, corporal punishment, expectations of childhood behaviours, and beliefs about children at work. New arrivals confront early childhood care and education systems conscribed by mandated policies and procedures built on cultural and social perspectives of child development as espoused by the majority in power, but also created by the requirement that is placed on these caregivers and educators to police the laws pertaining to the young and very young.

In their new communities, refugee and asylum-seeker families from other parts of the world find themselves challenged by the laws that regulate the roles of even the very young in the family. They may find that practices in child-rearing, while common in their homelands, are unacceptable or illegal. Laws in many Western, English-speaking countries prohibit young children being left unsupervised, entrusted into the care of a sibling or other young person who is not legally considered to be an adult. The degree of nurture and care provided in the home (and elsewhere) is measured against the standards of the new homeland, irrespective of the beliefs, backgrounds, family structures, and personal circumstances of the families in question (Lewig et al., 2010). Many English-speaking countries, among others, legislate strongly against the use of corporal punishment, and related discipline practices. This not only contra-dicts the perspectives of some cohorts responsible for the socialisation of their children (Renteln, 2010), but also a perspective which may be reinforced on their refugee journeys by the teachers in refugee camp schools (Fabbri et al., 2023; Fabbri et al., 2021).

The abolition of corporal punishment leaves many families without alter-native strategies with regard to setting boundaries and managing their chil-dren's undesirable behaviours (Bradley & Sellars, 2021) as the psychological strategies that are commonly used in many households are unfamiliar and the impact is not immediately apparent. While the notion of physically punishing young children who have already experienced displacement and trauma may appear abhorrent in itself, it may also lead to long-term social and psychologi-cal harm, increase children's feelings of anxiety, and lend itself to exclusionary practices in educational contexts (Mendenhall et al., 2021). The most critical aspect for refugee families engaging with childcare and education services, which are bound by the policies and laws of the new homeland regarding what constitutes developmentally appropriate activities for young children, acceptable child-rearing practices, and interfamily relationships, is that there is no room for integration. Assimilation is mandatory (Berry, 1997, 2001). In most circumstances and situations, diverse cultural and social perspectives about child development and associated activities are not tolerated, are illegal, or are exclusionary, even for the youngest of children. This may be particularly difficult for many parents and caregivers to accept, given that these interper-sonal relationship beliefs are deeply submerged in the subconscious and are emotionally highly charged (Hall, 1976).

Research findings

Resettlement workers from two large US cities recounted occasions where refugee families' parenting practices were strongly at odds with Western no-tions of appropriate and acceptable practice. In their telling, these educators attributed the parenting behaviours they observed to these families' cultures of origin, to the chaos and trauma these parents and families had experienced in their journeys to their new homelands, compounded by the pervasive violence in many refugee families' lives.

> *Context:* I work for a resettlement agency that has helped to resettle hundreds of refugees, asylees, and other vulnerable immigrants in [an American city in the midwest]. We have worked extensively with families from the Democratic Republic of Congo, from Burundi, Rwanda, Tanzania, Afghanistan, Iraq and Nepal. Our agency helps to place children into free pre-kindergarten programs and works to find affordable childcare to allow refugee parents to find work. The agency couples these services with orientations to key components of the systems of support that refugee families will need to navigate in their new community, including the law, employment, health, and education.

> I received a call from one particular center that they had brought in a translator because of some behaviour issues with the child. When I arrived, the mum was just getting on to their child and just letting them know what's up, up and down, and there was all sorts of stuff. The translator is like translating all of the things that she is saying, and she is just saying, 'if you don't behave, I'm going to set this black dog on you and let this black dog chew you up ...' and all of this and the child was just like distraught and burst into tears and all of this stuff.

> In some situations, our work is to figure out how to partner with the parent to help address concerns with their child's behavior [in a way that is acceptable in our society and under our laws]. In many cases, this is more about helping them get to the root of the behaviour issue itself and help to modify behaviors in the classroom. At the same time, we also prioritize educating parents about what is considered appropriate discipline [in the United States], what that looks like, and what we will be required to report to Child Protective Services, and different things like that.

> *Context:* We started a nursery and a pre-K program (in a large American city) to run concurrent to our adult education classes. With a grant from the federal government Office of Refugee Resettlement, we have been able to hire cultural brokers who are members of the refugee community, who we employed to do essentially case management services. I have worked with families from a dozen different nations.

> Because we hire people from the community to do most of our work, we're pretty culturally sensitive, it's baked into what we do. At the same time, we don't really worry about cultural differences unless they create legal issues. For example, it is critical that parents understand what you are and are not allowed to do regarding hitting your kids. That's an uncomfortable

conversation to have. We have police officers who come to our meetings with parents to deliver those conversations. We recognize what our expertise is, and where we are not the experts, and we bring experts in to discuss critical topics where we are not the experts, lawyers, police, psychologists. We are not mental health experts. We help the mental health experts understand the refugee experience, and they help us understand how to provide mental health support for these families.

Unique contexts, global principles

The refugee resettlement staff who spoke with us underscored the importance of ensuring families understand the boundaries around acceptable discipline in their new host countries, in order to keep them out of trouble with the law. As our refugee resettlement worker suggests, a mother threatening her young child with a vicious dog was bound to raise alarms for the educators and care staff in the room, who are also mandated by the state to report suspected cases of child abuse or neglect. All of this societal and cultural context would almost certainly have been unknown to the mother at the time. Our participant offered a measured response, ensuring the young mother understood that such threats are unacceptable in the host country, and that they actually might precipitate a visit from law enforcement or child protective services. Further, and consistent with conceptions of trauma-informed practice, our respondent saw an opportunity to work with the mother to determine why her child was acting out in class. Our second resettlement worker talked of the need to inform parents about the legal issues at play with hitting children in the US context. Having police officers, psychologists, and lawyers deliver the message enabled her to receive the information alongside her stakeholders (rather than deliver it) and added credibility and importance to the message. Of note, this participant was clear about deferring to experts wherever possible in the complex work of supporting children with refugee experiences. Across our research, participants represented a broad range of perspectives and contexts, including early care and learning centres and refugee resettlement agencies operating in very different communities across the Western societies in our study. These providers are similar in that they are working with young children and families that are navigating refugee and migrant experiences. Yet, more broadly, the settings, experiences, and individuals they spoke of underscore the variation within the broad category of migrant and asylee families. These examples illustrate the ways that families are very much on unique journeys from their places of origin to their new homes.

Professionals working with young children and families with refugee resettlement experiences may encounter parenting practices far different from Western notions of appropriate discipline. Educators may, as evidenced by our research, understand parents' behaviours as reflections of their home cultures, or of the chaos and trauma parents experienced in their journeys to their new homelands, or of experiences of violence in their own lives. Whatever their sources, the implications of these differences in beliefs about appropriate dis-cipline are significant for early childhood educators, who may find themselves in an uneasy position of having to navigate, interpret, and translate the under-standings and expectations of their new host societies to newly arrived families. Where to begin? For those who own or manage childcare centres, preschools, and playgroups, accessing experts to help staff develop both an understanding of acceptable and legal practices related to child-rearing and a rich knowledge of each family served by the organisation is vital. Gaining insights into cultural differences in child-rearing practices, learning about migration experiences and current living situations, may provide staff with helpful insights into the behaviours of children and the expectations of their parents.

Cultural notions of childhood

There are two major cultural perspectives surrounding the nature of childhood in addition to the multiple theories of child development (see, for example, Ertmer & Newby, 2013; Langford, 2005; Saracho, 2023; Washbrook et al., 2012; Wise & De Silva, 2007; Zuengler & Miller, 2006). These related to the distinguishing social and cultural traits that are identified in various countries Hofstede (2001, 2011). Hofstede et al. (2010) identified five differences in culture that are expressed as dimensions of culture. These were later added to by Minkov et al. (2017). Hofstede and his colleagues differentiate between English-speaking Western societies, such as those included in this research, and many eastern cultures, in terms of their *individualist* and *collectivist* di-mensions. Individualist cultures and societies emphasise the need for children to become as self-reliant and independent as their development stage allows, while collectivist cultures encourage children's continuing dependence on oth-ers in the group to which they belong. This societal difference has significant impact on their interactions in early years learning and caring contexts when the childcaring practices of home cultures appear contrary to those of the carer and educator beliefs and expectations. It is useful to note, however, that most societies fall somewhere along a continuum between the two paradigms. For example, Hofstede and his colleagues identify collectivist dimensions within some Western countries, such as Spain and those with Hispanic roots. They placed China, Vietnam, Malaysia, Thailand, Afghanistan, and Iran further to-wards the collectivist end of the scale. Conversely, Italy and Argentina are identified as individualist countries, but less so than the Anglo societies of Australia, Britian, or especially the United States, which strongly identifies as an individualist culture. These cultural distinctions quickly become evident in the context of early childhood care and development.

Opposing views on what babies and young children could or should do become apparent in some of the most basic actions that are part of everyday routines. Bedtime and sleeping routines are one example. In many collectivist cultures, including many countries throughout Southern Europe, Asia, Africa, and Central and South America, it is considered natural and appropriate to have babies and young children co-sleep in their parents' bed. Separating the infant or young child from the parent is considered unacceptable. Yet this is exactly the practice that is encouraged in many highly individualist cultures (Johnson et al., 2013). In these more individualistic societies, babies' rooms are prepared months before the new baby arrives. Newborns and infants may remain in the parents' room for some months, though usually in a cot or crib, separate from the adults and this arrangement is considered to be more of convenience for overnight nursing and diaper changes rather than a desire to have co-sleeping arrangements between parents and children. In individualist cultures, this becomes the beginning of the development of self-reliance and independence. For refugee and asylum-seeking mothers from more collectivist societies, having babies and toddlers sleep independently, and having their nap times interspersed in daytime activities may be problematic. In countries which may have some individualistic traits but are simultaneously heavily family-orientated, such as Argentina and Italy, small children and babies traditionally do not have early bedtimes but are included in the evening and late night activities enjoyed by the rest of the family. This may also create some difficulties in timetabling and scheduling of out-of-home environments for educators, carers, and tired children and babies.

How babies and young children are fed in regard to their independence, preferences, and choices is another cultural component that may present challenges in English-speaking countries with high scores on the individualist dimension of culture. As collectivist cultures deliberately cultivate this interdependence, believing it encourages the development of respect, patience, appreciation for others, and cultural and familial belonging, many babies and toddlers are spoon-fed until the time they begin school. This is in direct contrast to the customary practices in countries which advocate practices of self-reliance and independence. There are innumerable English language websites that provide step-by-step advice and video instruction on how to train babies and toddlers to feed themselves. These babies and toddlers are generally encouraged as soon as possible to pick up proportioned food in their hands, to use it as a tactile experience, to hold a spoon, and hopefully to manage to get some food into their mouths. In individualistic societies, self-feeding is regarded as an important aspect of child development, facilitating the development of fine motor skills, sensory perceptions, and hand–eye coordination and allowing babies and toddlers opportunity to exercise choice: a cornerstone of individualist societies. In this way babies and toddlers control how much they eat and how fast they want to eat. The complications for child carers and early educators are apparent. It is difficult to feed numerous children simultaneously and keep the food hot and/or palatable. The infants and children may not be able to eat sufficient food in the scheduled mealtimes and become hungry or undernourished, reflecting a need for schedules and control over time, which is a characteristic of many individualistic societies, placing an emphasis on planning and time keeping. Self-feeding may also lead to complaints from many parents who may, due to their previous experiences, have strong beliefs about the critical value of food and deplore their children's attempts to feed themselves, as food is not to be played with or wasted.

Toilet training practices provide another example of an arena in which social and cultural differences may create challenges for early care and learning providers working with young refugee children (JAVO et al., 2004). These issues also impact on contexts outside the home. Individualist cultures tend to encourage parents to wait until the child can get on the potty by themselves, are physiologically and emotionally ready and show interest (Kiddoo, 2012).

Numerous English language webpages provide advice and suggestions for parents on how to encourage the child to become active and interested in toilet training themselves. The usual recommended age is between 18 months and 2 years of age. Suggestions include allowing the toddlers to select their own potty when shopping, allowing them to investigate it by sitting on it, and even providing parents with suitable language for explaining its purpose to the child. Again, the focus is on independence, choice, and self-reliance.

On the other hand, in collectivist cultures, toilet training tends to start very early, usually about two to three weeks old and is wholly dependent at that stage upon the carers. Kiddoo (2012) describes this as elimination training and, at its most basic, carers are responsible initially for picking up the cues that babies give when they need to urinate or defecate. This is frequently facilitated by the close contact that many babies in these societies have with their mothers, who keep them in close contact by holding them or otherwise strapping them to themselves while they undertake their daily routines. As they begin to develop an accurate understanding of these cues, the babies may be held over a toilet at the relevant times, dispensing with the need for nappies (diapers). To facilitate a speedy response to their child's toileting needs, parents in China, for instance, traditionally dress their babies and toddlers in open crotch pants called 'kaidangku' (Carteret, 2016). This is still common practice in many provinces. This method relies on the cooperation and communication of the adult and child. Children may be trained to toilet on demand by parents and caregivers who use a specific prompting sound that they have created for use at these times. In this manner, elimination toilet training also becomes a co-dependent activity for which adults are responsible, unlike the stress on independently orientated toileting common in other cultures. This method may be more ecologically sensitive and sustainable but is impossible to achieve successfully with multiple babies and children in care and educational contexts.

Research findings

Across national contexts, participants in our research identified the inherent tension between Western, individualist, notions of best practices in early care and education and competing understandings of child development held by refugee families who arrive from more collectivist societies. The following observations from early childhood professionals in Australia and the United States underscore cultural differences in conceptions of early childhood development, with implications for the care of young children.

Context: Over the past twenty years, I've had the chance to work with many young children from refugee and migrant families [to Australia]. One thing that I've seen over that time is the difference between Western and non-Western ideas about the importance of developing individual autonomy in early childhood (and even later):

Self-help skills are highly valued in Western, Anglo societies. This is very much part of our culture where we talk about things like building grit and determination. But this focus on self-reliance is not so much a part of some other cultures. I remember a child who was fed by spoon by his Grandma for every meal until he was maybe four years of age. In that culture and family, the belief was that 'we need our child to be a very close part of our family' and we are not focused on their becoming independent. Leaving home? Eventually ... maybe. But certainly not when you turn 18, as in some countries. This isn't something you would do until you're 25 or married, right? In this respect, families' values and childrearing practices can be very different across cultures.

Context: Our centre [in Australia] is funded by the government to provide free childcare to migrant and refugee families who are coming to Australia on a permanent visa. This program is run by a well-established and reputable social service organization with over 125 years of experience providing childcare across Australia:

One conversation I find myself having (mostly with families from parts of Asia) concerns what is developmentally appropriate and how young children need to develop the capacity to engage in certain basic tasks. In practice, many of our parents need to stop feeding their youngest ones by three years of age. Don't spoon feed them. In preparation for these children transitioning to more formal school settings, I would like them to be able to put on their own shoes and socks. No one's going to do that for them when they go to preschool. From a Western perspective, these families really over-pamper their children.

Context: The two stories shared by our Australian colleagues contrast markedly with the following anecdote, shared by a respondent from a southern American city who has worked for three decades with children and families resettled to the community by international resettlement agencies. Many of these children are from families dislocated by wars and famines across Africa.

We were doing a home visit at the home of a Somali family. When we arrived, mom was still away at work, and the 4-year-old in charge. She was at the stove, making scrambled eggs for her 2-year-old brother who was in her care for the morning. A 4-year old babysitting, unsupervised, using the stove and a sharp knife ... these are unsettling things from a Western perspective, but are much more the norm in some African cultures.

Unique contexts, global principles

The examples shared by our respondents underscore the ways in which early childhood development is understood through different cultural lenses. Should early childhood development be understood in the context of the young child as an individual, or as a member of a family and community? This fundamental question may not be acknowledged by either families or care providers, but it is likely to colour many of their interactions. Without recognising these underlying differences in perspective, many components of early childhood development, including feeding and toileting practices, can become contested grounds. These everyday practices can be freighted with cultural understandings of how children develop, acceptable parenting practices, and suitable roles of early childhood educators. Our Australian respondents spoke of the cognitive dissonance between families who perceived young children as wholly dependent on the care of their kin far longer than is customary in the West and care providers who felt they had an obligation to strengthen their young students' development of autonomy. These anecdotes stand in marked contrast to the story shared by our American respondent, of a young child left in charge of her even younger sibling. Side by side, these stories indicate the broad range of cultural understandings of childhood.

Many young children spend more of their waking hours with care providers than they do with their own parents. And early childhood represents one of the most critical periods of brain development, when children's brains are literally becoming wired to respond to the stimuli in their lives. These roles are made even more complex when the children in care come from families that do not share Western beliefs about appropriate parenting practices, have different ideas about the place of children in the family, and may not accept Western notions about the need to encourage a child's developing a sense of autonomy and self-reliance. Educators working with young children in refugee families need to understand that understandings of childhood and appropriate early childhood development exist on a cultural continuum. When parents and educators approach child development from the vantage of different cultural constructs, there is a prospect for both conflict and learning. Educators carry a responsibility to consider these cultural differences in the families and children they serve. Meanwhile, helping families understand what is culturally acceptable in their new homes is a vital part of their work as well.

Bronfenbrenner's dilemma

Returning to the story that opens this chapter, the psychologist Urie Bronfenbrenner found himself at a loss to answer questions about individual children's development, despite his considerable professional expertise. The problem, Skolnick suggests, was perhaps due to the unit of analysis in Bronfenbrenner's work. In his Ecological Systems Theory, Bronfenbrenner (1976, 1979; Bronfenbrenner & Morris, 2006) gleaned insights into the beliefs and norms of families from the interrogation of entire cohorts of similarly placed people. The nature of this work precluded consideration of individual diversity within the larger social or cultural group. Similar consideration must be given to Hofstede (2011) in both his early and later collaborative analyses of the dimensions of culture. This is also pertinent to the interpretation of the Cultural Iceberg model (Hall, 1976) which contributed considerable insight into the interpersonal and intrapersonal relationships that develop because of the influence of cultural mores, values and beliefs, and the degree to which these are embedded in the consciousness of individuals as a whole.

These 'big picture' models can provide an overview of the ways in which people from different geographical and social backgrounds and experiences understand childhood and, in turn, how they believe children should be raised to become effective members of society. It gets more complicated when societal and cultural mores change; for example, when families find themselves confronting different laws governing discipline, or when they face different cultural beliefs about co-sleeping, self-feeding, or toilet training babies and toddlers. These challenges are felt most keenly by parents and caregivers of refugee and asylum-seeker young children, who may already have their parenting competencies undermined by their own trauma, poor mental and physical health, circumstances related to displacement, injury, and loss, and other resettlement difficulties.

As Bronfenbrenner concedes, theory only goes so far. Supporting the development of young children in refugee families means that care providers are responding to the needs of the individual families who make their way to the centre doors. While 'big picture' theories can help to capture the commonalities within the group, they are inadequate for understanding the differences within that group. Flexibility is important, as are models or guidelines for childcare centres and early educational settings. Importantly, this flexibility needs to be set inside a set of guidelines or model of reference or reflection, such as the SCARF model (Rock, 2008; Sellars, 2017, 2021, 2022; Sellars M & Imig S, 2021). It is only by reflecting on the personal values, principles, and mores that are embedded in many childcare and educational practices with a critical lens that the challenges, conflicts, and differences that exist at all levels – systemic, institutional, and personal (Brooks & Watson, 2019) – can be negotiated respectfully and with dignity for all individuals.

Research findings

In order to respond effectively to the needs of refugee and asylee families, it is vital that centre leadership and teachers work to establish a foundation of trust, and seek to be sensitive to the individual situation and unique needs of families. The following reflections from respondents in Australia and the United States provide helpful perspectives when it comes to navigating cultural perspectives and individual lived experiences.

> *Context:* I've had a lot of experience in different areas, working in the early childhood field, owning and operating my own early childhood centre (in a large American city), working as a University faculty member, and working with governments to establish teacher education policy.

> Essentially, it takes mentoring and coaching by the leadership, the administration of the Center to make sure teachers are honoring what those parents do, honoring the fact those parents make a choice. Even if the choice they make isn't what you consider typical, it must be honored, unless a child is actually in danger. So parents need to understand that they were listened to and their preferences were acknowledged. In those instances where the teacher felt like she knew better for this baby I had to say: 'You don't know better; you know differently, but you don't know better;' that's a hard thing for some of our teachers to accept: that there are cultural differences surrounding many of these issues and more than one legitimate perspective to consider.

> *Context:* Our centers are partnered with adult migrant English programs. We support migrants and refugee families around Australia to learn English at English colleges. We provide childcare on-site at the English colleges, or if we can't do that, we find a different mainstream centre for them. We have been funded by the Department of Home Affairs for 36 years now.

> I would want to tell beginning teachers: 'Do not make assumptions.' Just because somebody comes from a particular country or speaks a certain language does not mean that they will have the same needs of some of the families that you had. Maybe, as you try to understand a new family you Google their culture and think: 'Oh, that's what they do in a particular country.' But that is stereotyping, that's a very shallow surface-type of approach, and there's lots of danger in that because each family is unique in its own right. Their story is unique and different... every single family has its own story, and what's very important for us is to listen and to try to find out more about that family. It is important to remember that the person in front of you might come from this particular country and speak this language, but they are so much more than that. That's how you start to

build a trusting relationship and help families on their journey: by trying to understand their story as well as their culture.

Context: Practical suggestions for a direction forward are offered by the director of a centre run by the Australian migrant English programs:

We see a lot of cultural differences. But we consider how we can make the centre and classroom mirror a home environment in a way while also allowing parents to begin to understand the environment their children will be in once they go to school. Now we have large carpets where children can be there, we make it clear the mothers can take their shoes off if they wish. In terms of toileting, there are some mothers that prefer us not to change nappies. They would like to come down and do that themselves. After a while, with the trust that is built over time, they tend to start accepting our involvement in that way. We can change a nappy with the Afghan culture. So, I've had a mother show me that before, it was as opportunity for her to teach me.

Unique contexts, global principles

Whether in the United States or Australia, these early educators spoke of the need to balance Western and non-Western conceptions of child development and appropriate care practices, and to also balance a macro-level understanding of cultural differences with a more granular understanding of the situation of individual children and the readiness of their families to engage with care staff from a position of trust. In the examples above, one centre director spoke of the importance of educating her staff to see beyond their own world view. Our second director encourages her staff to learn about the families in their care, and to look beyond broad assumptions about whole cultures or nationalities. Meanwhile, our third educator suggested an opportunity to build understanding and trust with families by 'flipping the script' and asking mothers to teach her how they prefer that their infants have their diapers changed. As a group, our respondents underscore the importance of centre staff not assuming that all members of a migrant group have had identical experiences and beliefs. Moreover, many of the centre personnel we spoke with are serving migrants from a number of different cultures. One director explained that she currently was working with families that spoke 15 different languages. The category of 'migrant and asylum-seeking children' is far from uniform, and the experiences of their families are diverse.

In order to respond effectively to the needs of refugee and asylee families, it is vital that centre leadership and teachers work to establish trusting relationships with families, acknowledge that there are different perspectives on child development and child-rearing that are culturally specific, and remain sensitive to the individual situations and unique needs of different families. To that end, centre staff need support and direction. Centre directors tell us that they seldom have much lead time to prepare their staff to receive cohorts of new migrants. This is all the more reason to seek out opportunities to partner with refugee resettlement agencies and community leaders in order to provide vital professional development for centre staff to help them understand new families and communities.

Conclusion

Our respondents shared their perspectives from a broad range of contexts: they bring insights gained from early care and learning centres, and from refugee resettlement agencies operating in very different communities across Western societies. At one level, these professionals are alike in that they work with young children in families that have experienced displacement and are starting a new chapter in their lives as resettled refugees. Yet more broadly, the cultural backgrounds and individual experiences of resettled families are unique and different. Their stories underscore the variation within the broad category of migrant and asylee families. These families are on unique journeys from their places of origin, through migrant and resettlement experiences, to new homes and communities.

Societal and cultural mores and expectations about child-rearing and family life are made concrete through legislation and they are supported by informal norms and beliefs about matters as diverse as co-sleeping, self-feeding, or toilet training babies and toddlers. Without making these differences transparent, and acknowledging that many cultural lenses are equally reasonable, arbitrary enforcement of Western regimes around child development can compound the trauma and, in turn, become another challenge to the mental and physical health of refugees who have already dealt with displacement, loss, and resettlement.

Early childhood educators find themselves in the role of helping children and families navigate between the cultural understandings they inherited and cultural understandings they now are being asked to embrace. This task is made all the more difficult by language barriers, limited opportunities for professional development, and the already heavy workload of practitioners responding to the myriad needs of classrooms full of children navigating the first years of life.

References

Berry, J. (1997). Immigration, acculturation, and adaptation. *Applied Psychology: An International Review*, 46(1), 5–68.

Berry, J. (2001). A psychology of immigration. *Journal of Social Issues*, 7(3), 615–631.

Bradley, M., & Sellars, M. (2021). Parent cafe reflections. In *Making a spectacle: Examining curriculum/pedagogy as recovery from political trauma* (pp. 183–189). Information Age Publishing.

Bronfenbrenner, U. (1976). The experimental ecology of education. *Teachers College Record, 78*, 157–204.

Bronfenbrenner, U. (1979). *The ecology of human development: Experiments by nature and design.* Harvard University Press.

Bronfenbrenner, U., & Morris, P. (2006). The bioecological model of human development. In W. Damon & R. Lerner (Eds.), *Handbook of child psychology: Theoretical models of human development* (pp. 793–828). John Wiley & Sons, Inc.

Brooks, J., & Watson, T. (2019). School leadership and racism: An ecological perspective. *Urban Education, 54*(5), 631–655. https://doi.org/10.1177/0042085918783821

Carteret, M. (2016). Culturally-based differences in child rearing practices.

Ertmer, P. A., & Newby, T. J. (2013). Behaviorism, cognitivism, constructivism: Comparing critical features from an instructional design perspective. *Performance Improvement Quarterly, 26*(2), 43–71. https://doi.org/10.1002/piq.21143

Fabbri, C., Powell-Jackson, T., Rodrigues, K., De Filippo, A., Kaemingk, M., Torrats-Espinosa, G., Leurent, B., Shayo, E., Barongo, V., & Devries, K. M. (2023). Understanding why EmpaTeach did not reduce teachers' use of violence in Nyarugusu Refugee Camp: A quantitative process evaluation of a school-based violence prevention intervention. *PLOS Global Public Health, 3*(6), e0001404.

Fabbri, C., Rodrigues, K., Leurent, B., Allen, E., Qiu, M., Zuakulu, M., Nombo, D., Kaemingk, M., De Filippo, A., Torrats-Espinosa, G., Shayo, E., Barongo, V., Greco, G., Tol, W., & Devries, K. M. (2021). The EmpaTeach intervention for reducing physical violence from teachers to students in Nyarugusu Refugee Camp: A cluster-randomised controlled trial. *PLOS Medicine, 18*(10), e1003808. https://doi.org/10.1371/journal.pmed.1003808

Hall, E. (1976). *Beyond culture.* Knopf Doubleday Publishing Group.

Hofstede, G. (2001). *Culture's consequences: Comparing values, behaviors, institutions and organizations across nations* (2nd ed.). Sage.

Hofstede, G. (2011). Dimensionalizing cultures: The Hofstede model in context. *Online Readings in Psychology and Culture, 2*, 1–26.

Hofstede, G., Hofstede, G. J., & Minkov, M. (2010). *Cultures and organisations: Software of the mind.* McGraw-Hill.

Javo, C., Rønning, J., & Heyerdahl, S. (2004). Child rearing in an indigenous Sami population in Norway: A cross-cultural comparison of parental attitudes and expectations. *Scandinavian Journal of Psychology, 45*, 67–78.

Johnson, L., Radesky, J., & Zuckerman, B. (2013). Cross-cultural parenting: Reflections on autonomy and interdependence *Pediatrics, 131* (4), 631–633.

Kiddoo, D. A. (2012). Toilet training children: When to start and how to train. *Canadian Medical Association Journal, 184*(5), 511–511. https://doi.org/10.1503/cmaj.110830

Langford, P. (2005). *Vygotsky's developmental and educational psychology* (1st ed.). Psychology Press.

Lewig, K., Arney, F., & Salveron, M. (2010). Challenges to parenting in a new culture: Implications for child and family welfare. *Evaluation and Program Planning, 33*(3), 324–332. https://doi.org/10.1016/j.evalprogplan.2009.05.002

Mendenhall, M., Cha, J., Falk, D., Bergin, C., & Bowden, L. (2021). Teachers as agents of change: Positive discipline for inclusive classrooms in Kakuma refugee camp. *International Journal of Inclusive Education, 25*(2), 147–165. https://doi.org/10.1080/13603116.2019.1707300

Minkov, M., Bond, M. H., Dutt, P., Schachner, M., Morales, O., Sanchez, C., Jandosova, J., Khassenbekov, Y., & Mudd, B. (2017). A reconsideration of Hofstede's fifth dimension: New flexibility versus monumentalism data from 54 countries. *Cross-Cultural Research*, 52(3), 309–333. https://doi.org/10.1177/1069397117727488

Renteln, A. (2010). Corporal punishment and the cultural defense. *Law and Contemporary Problems*, 73(Spring), 253–279.

Rock, D. (2008). SCARF: A brain-based model for collaborating with and influencing others. *NeuroLeadership Journal*, 1, 1–9.

Saracho, O. N. (2023). Theories of child development and their impact on early childhood education and care. *Early Childhood Education Journal*, 51(1), 15–30. https://doi.org/10.1007/s10643-021-01271-5

Sellars, M. (2017). *Reflective practice for teachers* (2nd ed.). Sage.

Sellars, M. (2021). Belonging and being: Developing inclusive ethos. *International Journal of Leadership in Education*. https://doi.org/10.1080/13603124.2021.1942994

Sellars, M. (2022). Radical acceptance: Teachers who support students with migrant, refugee, and asylum seeker backgrounds. *Teachers and Teaching*, 29(5), 528–541. https://doi.org/10.1080/13540602.2022.2098269

Sellars, M., & Imig, S. (2021). School leadership, reflective practice, and education for students with refugee backgrounds: A pathway to radical empathy. *Intercultural Education*, 1–13. https://doi.org/10.1080/14675986.2021.1889988

Skolnick, A. (1975). The limits of childhood: Conceptions of child development and social context. *Law and Contemporary Problems*, 39(3), 38–77.

Washbrook, E., Waldfogel, J., Bradbury, B., Corak, M., & Ghanghro, A. A. (2012). The development of young children of immigrants in Australia, Canada, the United Kingdom, and the United States. *Child Development*, 83(5), 1591–1607. https://doi.org/10.1111/j.1467-8624.2012.01796.x

Wise, S., & De Silva, L. (2007). *Differential parenting of children from diverse cultural backgrounds attending child care*. Canberra: Commonwealth of Australia.

Zuengler, J., & Miller, E. R. (2006). Cognitive and sociocultural perspectives: Two parallel SLA worlds? *TESOL Quarterly*, 40(1), 35–58. https://doi.org/10.2307/40264510

Chapter 5

Play supports social, emotional, and cognitive development

Introduction

Child psychologist Jean Piaget observed: 'play is the work of children.' Or, as American children's television host Fred Rogers put it, 'Play is often talked about as if it were a relief from serious learning. But for children, play is serious learning.' For children who are caught up in the chaos and uncertainty confronting many families with refugee or asylum-seeker experiences, opportunities for play can be overlooked. This chapter offers insights into the importance of play for child development, and its role in supporting early childhood development for young children from newly arrived families. The chapter includes reflections from professionals on how to create opportunities for young children to experience the joys of play, and suggestions for introducing sceptical parents to play-based early childhood curricula.

What is play?

Dismissing a task for adults as 'child's play' misrepresents the importance and purpose of play in a child's life. This is particularly true in the early childhood years, as play literally helps build the architecture of a child's developing brain. Through play, babies and young children begin to learn about the world around them and about themselves, learn to communicate, and gain mastery of important concepts. Through play, babies, toddlers, and young children are able to demonstrate developmental milestones, explore and engage with their environments, and express their inner worlds as actions and behaviours. In fact, Woolley (2021) asserts the child's right to play is one that is overlooked in times of war and other disasters, despite its critical importance in children's well-being and development. Anderson-McNamee and Bailey (2010) offer an explanation of the different types of play and the stages of development at which they each may be engaged in as understood in Western cultures. These stages are not age based but may be very roughly correlated with periods of growth and skill development in environments which are supportive of babies, toddlers, and young children without disadvantages or disease. They assert

DOI: 10.4324/9781003404231-6

that the random movements and explorations of space in which babies up to three months are engaged are actually the beginnings of play identified as *unoccupied play*. This is generally followed by an extended period of *solitary play* as babies and toddlers up to about 18 months habitually play alone, are frequently oblivious to others playing near them. This solitary play is considered to be an important capacity for children to develop, resulting as it does from the limited social, physical, and cognitive skills that typify this stage of development. Commencing from about 18 months of age, toddlers may engage with *onlooker play* where they watch others play without attempting to engage with the play themselves. These occasions are frequently opportunities to listen and develop language associated with the activities and may be engaged with at any stage of development. *Parallel play* may often be observed as toddlers aged 18 months to 2 years play alongside each other without actually interacting with each other. It may provide opportunities for toddlers to engage in imaginative play and to develop the concept of ownership, frequently using the word 'mine.'

After the age of approximately three years, toddlers may gradually engage in *associative* and *social play*. Associative play implies that the toddlers are more interested in other children than they are in the toys provided to play with. They are beginning to develop some social skills, including how to share, how to get along with others during play, and how to play together with a common purpose. They may select to play with the same toys, exchange one toy for another's, and generally just play together. Associative play is unstructured play. It has no rules or formal organisation, rather it provides opportunities for language development, problem-solving, and cooperation. Social play, in contrast, while emerging in approximately the same period of time, has a particular aspect that distinguishes it from associative play. Also social in nature, social play is distinguished by the introduction of the child's sense of moral reasoning about values such as fairness, taking turns, and being negotiation. Social play in diverse contexts allows the child to develop these skills and to understand the flexibility of different situations. Many activities throughout these stages of development, and later, involve *physical play*. Jumping, running, crawling, and other activities involving movement allow for the development of gross motor skills, social skills such as winning or losing, and sound spatial awareness. The *constructive component of play* is also observable during these types of play, from the early stages of babies experimenting by putting things in their mouths through to the actual manipulating, building, and construction of objects. *Expressive play* is also found throughout the different types of play. Babies, toddlers, and young children learn to use language, media, and a wide range of artefacts to express their feelings and develop a range of fine and gross motor skills, pattern, and rhythm. It is in *fantasy play* that children of any age assume identities and roles other than their own. They may dress up, mimic adult behaviours, and think abstractly to fulfil their new roles. *Cooperative play* is exactly that. It depends on a group working together to make the play enjoyable, is more formal in nature, and has a leader. Cooperative play skills are usually developed from about four years onwards as young children may experience the later years of preschool or the early years of schooling. Throughout these various types of play, there are multiple opportunities for vocabulary and language development, for engaging with increasingly complex cognitive skills, for engaging in social and emotional development by learning about oneself and others, and for developing physical skills and capacities (Charles & Bellinson, 2019).

Research findings

In spite of the importance of play to early childhood development, it may be unfamiliar to young children from families with refugee experiences. Many of these children arrive at early childhood centres with play skills far less developed than their same-age peers. Teachers in Australia and the United States shared stories of introducing children and their families to play.

> *Context:* Early childhood educators offered strikingly parallel stories of needing to introduce play to newly arrived children and their families. An educator from New South Wales tells of working with children from African families while their parents were engaged in life skills training at a local church.

> One of the things we have to be sensitive to is the need to teach some children how to play. Some of these kids really and truly don't know how to play, they may never have had the experience of just running around outside, or simply having the chance to engage in play. It's quite an interesting concept.

> Some children, and their families, frankly, need the chance to learn how to be comfortable with unstructured play. And, so we direct them to other opportunities like supported playgroups, where they can engage with other migrant families and their children can play together. Not only does this experience provide a bit of community for these families, and the chance for their children to develop their ability to play, but it is also an environment where they can feel welcomed and safe, and secure.

> *Context:* I have over 35 years of working with refugee and migrant children (in the US). One of the themes I have seen repeatedly is a level of discomfort with our emphasis on play. Many of our parents do not (at least immediately) see the ways in which play in early childhood is a foundation for school readiness across many domains of development.

> Everything about early childhood learning and development should be through play. Our center has a no-screen policy. I know I lost many families because of that. Families wanted to see computers in the center, but I said no. No computers, no iPads. We do have iPads available for special projects, like

if all the kids came up with questions and they wanted to do research. Like if they'd ask about how tadpoles become frogs, or something like that, we'd get out the iPad and be able to look that up. But, as a general rule, as part of the regular day, no. And, I think screen time is just a detriment, and so I really feel like we have to get back to a stronger emphasis on play as the foundation of learning. I think preschool should be fundamentally about learning to play as a group.

Unique contexts, global principles

Few of the themes addressed in this project elicited as strong a level of agreement among the early childhood educators as the fundamental role of play for early childhood learning and development. That foundational role is supported by research in child development, and is reflected in the play-based curricula that have been adopted across the national-contexts in which our conversations occurred. Yet the importance of play to early childhood development may be unfamiliar to many families with refugee backgrounds, who understand schooling to be heavily structured and oriented towards academic discipline. As our Australian participant observed, it is not unusual for newly arrived children and their parents to need to be taught how to play. And, as our American respondent noted, it is no wonder that these families would have some level of discomfort with the emphasis on play within centres, and with their intentional disregard for computers and other 'screens' that will be central to learning later in life.

Through their reflections, these educators underscore the importance of recognising the potential unease that newly arrived parents may have with play-based curricula. (In fact, many educators we interviewed work in regions where there are parent groups pushing against play-based curricula as they see it as a diversion from *rigorous* academics.) Our participants also underscored the important role that centres have in creating opportunities for children and their parents to learn not only *how to* play, but also *why* to play. For families that have come from countries where play is seen as a frivolity, the work of educators is much more challenging and important.

Play and society

While play may be established in terms of educational and developmental value, it is also important to consider the meaning and value of play in diverse societal, sociological, and cultural contexts (Göl-Güven, 2017). The current neoliberal emphasis on Western education systems has resulted in the reconceptualisation of the role of play in many of the geographical areas of the world where the nature and potential of play had been historically recognised by the founding pedagogues of modern education (Garwood, 1982; Marshall, 2017; Saracho & Spodek, 1995; Sellars & Imig, 2020). The culture of performance, testing, measuring, and benchmarking is not conducive to play, even in the realms of many early childcare environments, preschool, and early years classrooms. Nicolopoulou (2010, p. 1) commented:

> Across the board, play is being displaced by a single-minded focus on teaching academic skills through direct instruction. This emphasis on more didactic, academic, and content-based approaches to preschool education comes at the expense of more child-centered, play-oriented, and constructivist approaches, which are dismissed as obsolete or simply crowded out.

This societal dismissal of play which reflects children's own worlds and interests as a somewhat less valued learning opportunity reflects the 'race to the top' mentality of many individualist cultures where competition, speed, personal achievement, and less tightly constructed social networks form the trademarks (Hofstede, 2001, 2011). The situation in Germany for example, the homeland of the term 'kindergarten,' appears to reflect the more functional approach to early childhood education, focusing on teaching of academic subjects in preparation for school than on the more traditional situated play (free play) or even structured play (Faas et al., 2017). This is in spite of the findings of a systematic review of research into the learning outcomes that were the result of play-based activities which indicated significant development in understanding language and literacy and mathematics.

The quality of the child's environment and their interactions within the contexts with which they engage have a significant impact on the child's learning (Bronfenbrenner, 1979; Bronfenbrenner & Morris, 2006). The interactions among and between systems and children as they grow and learn are not simple one-to-one interactions and largely depend on the richness and complexity of these environmental systems and the people of which they comprise (Maher & Buxton, 2015). They are the ways in which children advance their thinking by accessing the cultural expertise of the adults in their environments by engaging in what Vygotsky termed the 'zone of proximal development' – the educational pathway that facilitates learning and growth of consciousness – in this case through play. Veraksa et al. (2022, p. 1) assert:

> For Vygotsky, the zone of proximal development is an important educator's tool for effectively influencing not only learning but even the formation of children's consciousness. It is particularly pertinent for early education as the emergent properties of the zone are evident not only in the process of instruction, but also of play, which forms the basis of early curricula around the developed world.
>
> (Organization for Economic Cooperation Development, 2017)

While the final statement may not ring true for many contexts in the 'developed world' despite the currency of the publication, the perspective offers confirmation of the importance of the play environment for children's learning, in terms of both physical operations and human interactions. Roopnarine (2012) and Roopnarine and Johnson (2001) refine this notion by suggesting that each social setting and cultural setting has its own set of cognitive and social values that, depending on various other conditions, may be encouraged in different types of play. These other variables may depend on immediate need, which is the need for the children to work in or for the household as soon as possible, the parental beliefs about the benefits of play, and the ways in which play is interpreted. The latter may lead to a greater understanding of the enculturation processes of fantasy play.

Research findings

Across contexts, our respondents emphasised the importance of play for early childhood development and underscored the special importance of play for children who have experienced the trauma of dislocation. At the same time, for many families with refugee experiences, play may appear trivial, or even an outright distraction from key school readiness skills. We spoke with centre directors in Australia and New Zealand who each offered insights about the challenge of introducing play to newly arrived families.

> *Context:* The child care centre I direct (in Australia) serves a student population overwhelmingly made up of English as a second language (ESL) students. Many of these children are from refugee families; Many have spent time in refugee camps; Many have come up on the illegal boats. Many of these families don't trust us, they don't trust Australians, and they don't trust leaving their children here. That mistrust extends to deep misgivings about the play-based nature of the centre's curriculum.
>
> We try to explain to families that we have play-based learning, which is different from formal Kindergarten schooling. Their children will apply what they learn here with us when they reach kindergarten. With us, they will learn how to count and that sort of stuff through play, and alongside their development of the social skills they will need through life, and how to build relationships and be independent. There has been some push back from parents in the past. We have had some families pull out, which is fine because there are a lot of other services that do offer the academic stuff. But for us, our free school is big on pure relationships, independence, that sort of stuff, and it's not a perfect fit for everyone, and that's fine as well. But yeah, always some pushback about it, parents' desire for a more rigorous, academic focus.
>
> *Context:* Our early childhood curriculum (in New Zealand) is called Te Whāriki, and it is underpinned by a vision of developing children who are healthy, secure, and competent learners and communicators, and it is heavily

play-based. At the same time, it is also our philosophy to embrace family and community engagement, and our early learning programs are designed in a way that allows each community, and each early learning service, to develop and design its daily practice based on the needs and the environment of the community. These perspectives (on play and on community-engagement) can be deeply difficult to reconcile in certain refugee communities that don't find value in play-based early learning environments.

A play-based early learning environment for early education is not acceptable and does not make sense to some cultures. We see this particularly with families from some Asian cultures, who are looking for a very straightforward, academic, basic education for their children. We need to explain that children who graduate from our program will go on to be academically successful, while also learning critical social, emotional and behavioral skills. Without those facets of their development, children will experience a shock when they need to interact with other children and teachers they encounter later in their education. Different cultures value what is the best education for the early years differently.

Unique contexts, global principles

The importance of play and the concept of play-based learning may be alien to families with refugee experiences. Our participants shared conversations they have had with parents looking for preschool to be a 'bootcamp' preparing their children for the rigors of K-12. Parents may have an expectation of early learning that is shaped by a different societal context: one in which play is, almost by definition, the opposite of formal schooling. These parents often want their preschoolers to have a more rigorous, academically oriented preschool experience. The role of play can become a contested issue when the perspectives it elicits are so opposed. In this respect, it also represents an opportunity for centres to find common ground with parents around shared goals (certainly including academic readiness). Our respondent from New Zealand was clear that educators need to help parents understand the academic and social, emotional and behavioural benefits of play-based learning.

Convincing parents of the importance of play-based learning is not an easy task, particularly when parents may approach the need to leave their children in out-of-home care with suspicion. As our Australian participant noted, trust is a major issue for newly arrived families and that mistrust can extend all the way to the type of education children are receiving. Again, our respondents speak to the foundational need to build trust between parents and early childhood educators as the way forward out of this dilemma. Centres have the imperative to create settings that encourage play and, when working with children with refugee backgrounds, to create opportunities for parents to participate in play-based learning as well.

Play and culture

Perspectives on play differ across cultural groups. These are complex and intertwined with the ideological and ethnological foundations upon which societies and their factions are built. Roopnarine and Davidson (2015) discuss the attempts made to develop a defining framework for interpreting play across cultures, including considering the impacts of individualist versus collectivist mainstream cultures (Hofstede, 2001, 2011; Hofstede et al., 2010). This appears to be a useful lens through which to interpret understandings and attitudes towards play, considering its impact on the diverse notions of childhood which are found globally. There are anomalies, however. The authors report Thai children being taught to be independent while very young, circumstances where the caregivers other than parents are facilitating play and in developing countries parents spent time with their children playing, mainly outside, but to a lesser degree than reported by parents in the United States. It may appear that Western parents are more inclined to see the value of child's play than non-Western parents, with mothers playing substantially more than fathers. However, the difficulty in determining the value of play across cultures is simply that the definitions, interpretations, and parameters of 'play' as applied by Western researchers are not necessarily reliable in determining the ways in which different types of play contribute to the cognition, socialisation, and communicative skills across cultures. Again, it may appear that assessing a fish on how effectively it might climb a tree is neither informative nor useful. Additionally, what may be reported to be valued may not actually reflect the beliefs of those entrusted to action the beliefs, as was evidenced in the Hong Kong study where early childhood policymakers determined that play was beneficial in the early years educational contexts but the early childhood educators, predominantly from Confusions epistemologies, separated the young children in formal classrooms from the age of three years and continued with prescribed instruction (Faas et al., 2017). The most informative way forward to better understand play across cultures may be exactly as suggested by Roopnarine (2012), Roopnarine and Davidson (2015), and Roopnarine and Johnson (2001): the development of indigenous theories, definitions, and values of play.

The sheer diversity of ethnicities, epistemologies, circumstances of displacement, degree of trauma, and pre-migration contexts of the babies, toddlers, young children, their families, and communities who have been resettled into the countries which are the focus of this study is overwhelming. What is useful to understand is that many will have some backgrounds of poverty and hardship, have been exposed to unspeakable violence of one type or another, have experienced danger and threat to their safety, and are surviving and settling in an entirely new world. The need for physical safety, especially around girls, may be the underlying reason that female refugee students did not draw pre-migration play experiences and drew their post-migration play experiences in outdoor contexts in a study conducted by Macmillan et al. (2015). While Western notions of play and its value for children's development may have misinterpretations and limitations, there are many useful aspects of these theories that may serve to support and heal these babies, toddlers, and young children and their communities. Play therapy and art therapy can make a significant contribution to the healing process (Hilado et al., 2021; Lau et al., 2018; Macmillan et al., 2015). Critical to the play interactions are safe, supportive environments with well-informed carers, a perspective central to the vision of Vygotsky who viewed the adult as the expert guide to culture. This has not always been possible in the pre-settlement lives of babies, children, and toddlers with refugee and asylum-seeker backgrounds.

While Heldal (2021) found the stress in the play environment provided in a refugee camp in Lesbos that she investigated using a salutogenic approach (Pastoor, 2017; Shakespeare-Finch et al., 2014) was totally cognisant of the importance of supporting children's play and acknowledging their feelings, ideas, and experiences as unique and valuable, this was not widespread. The *Child Friendly Spaces* (CFSs) is a recognised child support initiative in many refugee camps; the study of another refugee kindergarten in Greece (Ardelean, 2021) found that a limited understanding of the nature and range of play activities by the early childcare teachers resulted in the children being engaged in highly controlled, limited activities identified as play which, when considered with the other restrictions of camp life in general, did not generate a supportive play environment for the children. Similarly, a high ratio of children to adults, inadequate resources, and insufficient carer professional development in a Durban childcare centre for young children with refugee experiences impacted negatively on their capacities to thrive (Adams-Ojugbele & Moletsane, 2019). However, a study of flexible early childhood programmes in Germany that were provided specially for young children with refugee and asylum-seeker experiences appear to have had more success with mothers attending playgroups with their children, although the structure of the play was not explored (Busch et al., 2023). While presenting more positive outcomes with babies, toddlers, and young children with refugee backgrounds aged 0–5 years and their parents, the philosophical and pedagogical underpinnings of the play activities in which the children were engaged were not described in detail by Hilado et al. (2021).

A number of participants in this study found the cultural differences on the importance of play as opposed to more direct instruction and formal learning to be challenging. In a study of (non-refugee) parental beliefs about the potential of play activities in preschools to promote the development of executive function skills (namely working memory, inhibition, and flexible memory), Metaferia et al. (2021) found considerable differences in the parental attitudes of parents in Hungary and Ethiopia. As a highly individualistic society (Hofstede, 2001; Geert Hofstede, 2011; Hofstede et al., 2010; Insights, 2023), Hungarian parents were supportive of preschool play activities, perceiving the goal of this educational stage was primarily the development of social and emotional skills. These children engaged in solitary play, fine motor, sport, and other physical activity after school. On the contrary, parents in the collective society of Ethiopia (Hofstede, 1986, 2011; Insights, 2023) understood the primary focus of preschool education as fostering academic skills, a finding congruent with other studies. These children spent their after-school hours engaging with arts and craft activities and academic tasks. While these researchers did not find any significant differences in the development of executive function skills, they did suggest that, as collective societies have a preference for modelling 'correct' behaviour as a means of integrating children into the group from the outset, toddlers were expected to model impulse regulation and inhibition as early as two years old. This is significantly earlier than is expected in individualist cultures and may explain the cultural differences in parental expectations of preschool activity as parents from collectivist societies as they have expectations that their very young children have the capacities to engage with formal learning contexts and content. The importance of play for socio-emotional development for students from collectivist cultures who have experienced trauma and/or depravation as the consequence of refugee and asylum-seeker backgrounds may be another challenge of cultural ontologies, given the diverse perceptions of mental health and emotional life across belief systems. As the question of the nature, purpose, and actualisation of purposeful play and learning activities for these babies, toddlers, and young children at risk remains relatively unclear from a cultural perspective, and given the increasing medical evidence of the relationship between emotion and cognition, what remains to be negotiated is the degree to which play experiences and learning activities have a positive impact on the social and emotional healing and academic development of individual children.

Research findings

Families who find themselves living in a new country bring with them long-held beliefs about the importance of education. Likewise, these families have views about the importance, or lack of importance, of play. We spoke with an early childhood educator in the United States and an educator in Australia who shared their experiences helping families understand the place of play in learning and culture.

> *Context:* I've been an early childhood educator for 22 years, including work with refugee children for many years. Play is important and, in particular, the use of toys, in working with children from families with refugee experiences, and with their associated trauma.
>
> I think play ... is very valuable, whether you're in a formal play therapy environment or not. Really, that's what the kids are doing naturally in the sandbox, or when they are playing together with the toys that are in the

center. So, one thing we can do is help teachers think of questions they can ask to encourage interactive play and to encourage positive interactions between the children. They might, for example, show the children the toys playing with each other in positive and supportive ways, modeling that behavior for the children. Again, this is a way for the adult to enter the play but not taking it over.

Context: I've spent many years working with young children in playgroup settings. I try to share the play-based lessons we are teaching in the classroom with parents. This allows parents to strengthen, replicate and enjoy this type of interactive play with their children at home.

We are really structured about interaction between adults and children. In that sense, it is so important that there is strong interaction from parent to child, what the developmental psychologists refer to as 'serve and return' interactions. So, we're working on that relationship. If that's not coming naturally for a parent, I support them by working on that. This could be something as simple as saying like, 'Let's go outside with the ball. Mom, you sit at that end, and Scotty, you sit at that end, and we're just going to roll the ball back and forth to each other.' That gets them connected straight away…It could be that when they're playing with a matchbox car, they roll the car back and forth, or I might say to the parent: As your child is playing, you could name what they're doing, like if they're building with blocks you can say: 'Ooh, you're building with the blocks now. I see your tower is really high!,' just something as simple as that, just sometimes giving parents the language that they can use in play, often that's enough of a prompt for them to think 'I can do that!' A fun family session for us with even 20 kids and their parents is to practice a little of that kind of interaction.

Unique contexts, global principles

Our respondents recognise that play-based learning is both vitally important, and yet is often unfamiliar (or even suspect) to many families with refugee or asylum-seeker experiences. These early childhood professionals emphasise the importance of creating a culture of early learning that privileges play and emphasise that this is particularly true for refugee children. This may extend to introducing a child to the concept of play itself. As more than one of our respondents noted, children may arrive at their centres without understanding the concept of play and, as a result, they have not had access to a vital arena of early childhood development. Beyond providing opportunities for play, our participants each talked about the purposeful work that educators can engage in around play. Our US educator models interactions between toys that offer young children an opportunity to witness collaboration and positive play. Our Australian educator suggests describing the play out loud as it provides young children and parents with a broader vocabulary and helps both engage with the experience.

As a group, our respondents describe their efforts to create cultures within their centres where play is celebrated and encouraged between students, between students and teachers, and between parents and children beyond the classroom, and where it extends to include opportunities for families to gather together under the broad umbrella of 'playgroups' for children. While providing young children with time for unstructured play is certainly important for learning environments, educators can be purposeful in developing practices around play to expand academic, social, and emotional learning.

Conclusion

Collectively, our respondents describe a vision of play-based learning that expands to include the child, classroom, family, and community. For the child who has been forcibly displaced, play becomes the pathway to engaging with the new and unfamiliar world around them, and – in the process – allows them to discover their place in that new world. Certainly, a core component of that discovery process is the development of interpersonal interactions and skills, including those between the child and their peers and between the child and their teachers. Many of those interactions take place through play, and they provide a portal through which teachers and other care providers, including mental health providers, can gain insight into the trauma children have experienced and offer a language through which teachers can help guide the development of their young charges. Beyond the classroom, our respondents spoke of the need to nurture a culture of play among newly arrived families. They are helping to build transparency and trust with parents, and they are helping parents understand the 'why' behind play-based learning. In so doing, they are also making clear that educators are also committed to the important goals of social, emotional, and cognitive readiness for school. Further, this expanded concept of a culture of play serves to create opportunities for parents to establish the 'serve and return' relationships with their children that developmental psychologists tell us are at the core of healthy child development. Finally, the efforts of many of our research participants to work through community agencies and to establish playgroups beyond the traditional classroom speaks to the ways this notion of a culture of play serves to further the bonds between recently arrived families, and strengthen their developing communities of support.

References

Adams-Ojugbele, R. O., & Moletsane, R. (2019). Towards quality early childhood development for refugee children: An exploratory study of a Grade R class in a Durban child care centre. *South African Journal of Childhood Education*, 9(1). https://doi.org/10.4102/sajce.v9i1.616

Anderson-McNamee, J., & Bailey, S. (2010). The importance of play in early childhood development. Montana State University Extension, pp. 1–4. Retrieved July 23, 2023, from https://www.montana.edu/extension/health/documents/MT201003HR.pdf

Ardelean, A. (2021). Play in a refugee camp: Disorder from chaos. *International Journal of Play*, *10*(4), 355–360. https://doi.org/10.1080/21594937.2021.20 05395

Bronfenbrenner, U. (1979). *The ecology of human development: Experiments by nature and design*. Harvard University Press.

Bronfenbrenner, U., & Morris, P. (2006). The bioecological model of human development. In W. Damon & R. Lerner (Eds.), *Handbook of child psychology: Theoretical models of human development* (pp. 793–828). John Wiley & Sons, Inc.

Busch, J., Buchmüller, T., & Leyendecker, B. (2023). Implementation and quality of an early childhood education program for newly arrived refugee children in Germany: An observational study. *International Journal of Child Care and Education Policy*, *17*(1). https://doi.org/10.1186/s40723-023-00105-8

Charles, M., & Bellinson, J. (Eds.). (2019). *The importance of play in early childhood education: Psychoanalytic, attachment, and developmental perspectives* (1st ed.). Routledge.

Faas, S., Wu, S.-C., & Geiger, S. (2017). The importance of play in early childhood education: A critical perspective on current policies and practices in Germany and Hong Kong. *Global Education Review*, *4*(2), 75–91.

Garwood, S. G. (1982). Piaget and play: Translating theory into practice. *Topics in Early Childhood Special Education*, *2*(3), 1–13. https://doi.org/10.1177/027112148200200305

Göl-Güven, M. (2017). Play and flow: Children's culture and adults' role. *Erken Çocukluk Çalışmaları Dergisi*, *1*(2), 267–281. https://doi.org/10.24130/eccd-jecs.196720171230

Heldal, M. (2021). Perspectives on children's play in a refugee camp. *Interchange*, *52*(3), 433–445. https://doi.org/10.1007/s10780-021-09442-4

Hilado, A., Chu, A., & Magrisso, A. (2021). Treatment for refugee children and their families. In J. D. Aten & J. Hwang (Eds.), *Refugee mental health* (pp. 215–250). American Psychological Association. https://doi.org/10.1037/0000226-009

Hofstede, G. (1986). Cultural differences in teaching and learning. *International Journal of Intercultural Relations*, *10*, 301–320.

Hofstede, G. (2001). *Culture's consequences: Comparing values, behaviors, institutions and organizations across nations* (2nd ed.). Sage.

Hofstede, G. (2011). Dimensionalizing cultures: The Hofstede model in context. *Online Readings in Psychology and Culture*, *2*, 1–26.

Hofstede, G., Hofstede, G. J., & Minkov, M. (2010). *Cultures and organisations: Software of the mind*. McGraw-Hill.

Lau, W., Silove, D., Edwards, B., Forbes, D., Bryant, R., McFarlane, A., Hadzi-Pavlovic, D., Steel, Z., Nickerson, A., Van Hooff, M., Felmingham, K., Cowlishaw, S., Alkemade, N., Kartal, D., & O'Donnell, M. (2018). Adjustment of refugee children and adolescents in Australia: Outcomes from wave three of the building a new life in Australia study. *BMC Medicine*, *16*(1), 157. https://doi.org/10.1186/s12916-018-1124-5

Macmillan, K. K., Ohan, J., Cherian, S., & Mutch, R. C. (2015). Refugee children's play: Before and after migration to Australia. *Journal of Paediatrics and Child Health*, *51*(8), 771–777. https://doi.org/10.1111/jpc.12849

Maher, M., & Buxton, L. (2015). Early childhood education at the cultural interface. *The Australian Journal of Indigenous Education*, *44*(1), 1–10. https://doi.org/10.1017/jie.2015.5

Marshall, C. (2017). Montessori education: A review of the evidence base. *npj Science of Learning*, *2*(1). https://doi.org/10.1038/s41539-017-0012-7

Metaferia, B. K., Futo, J., & Takacs, Z. K. (2021). Parents' Views on Play and the Goal of Early Childhood Education in Relation to Children's Home Activity and Executive Functions: A Cross-Cultural Investigation. Front Psychol, 12, 646074. https://doi.org/10.3389/fpsyg.2021.646074

Nicolopoulou, A. (2010). The alarming disappearance of play from early childhood education. *Human Development*, *53*(1), 1–4. https://doi.org/10.1159/000268135

Pastoor, L. d. W. (2017). Reconceptualising refugee education: Exploring the diverse learning contexts of unaccompanied young refugees upon resettlement. *Intercultural Education*, *28*(2), 143–164. https://doi.org/10.1080/14675986.2017.1295572

Organization for Economic Cooperation and Development (2017). Starting Strong 2017—Key OECD Indicators on Early Childhood Education and Care. New York, NY: OECD Publishing. doi: 10.1787/9789264276116-en

Roopnarine, J. L. (2012). What is the state of play? *International Journal of Play*, *1*(3), 228–230. https://doi.org/10.1080/21594937.2012.735452

Roopnarine, J. L., & Davidson, K. (2015). Parent–child play across cultures advancing play research. *The American Journal of Play*, *7*(2), 228–248.

Roopnarine, J. L., & Johnson, J. E. (2001). Play and diverse cultures: Implications for early childhood education. In S. Reifel & M. H. Brown (Eds.), *Early education and care, and reconceptualizing play* (Vol. 11, pp. 295–319). Emerald Group Publishing Limited. https://doi.org/10.1016/S0270-4021(01)80012-4

Saracho, O. N., & Spodek, B. (1995). Children's play and early childhood education: Insights from history and theory. *Journal of Education*, *177*(3), 129–148. https://doi.org/10.1177/002205749517700308

Sellars, M., & Imig, D. (2020). Pestalozzi and pedagogies of love: Pathways to educational reform. *Early Child Development and Care*, *191*, 1152–1163. https://doi.org/10.1080/03004430.2020.1845667

Shakespeare-Finch, J., Schweitzer, R. D., King, J., & Brough, M. (2014). Distress, coping, and posttraumatic growth in refugees from Burma. *Journal of Immigrant & Refugee Studies*, *12*(3), 311–330. https://doi.org/10.1080/15562948.2013.844876

Vasiou, A., Kassis, W., Krasanaki, A., Aksoy, D., Favre, C. A., & Tantaros, S. (2023). Exploring parenting styles patterns and children's socio-emotional skills. *Children*, *10*(7), 1126. https://doi.org/10.3390/children10071126

Veraksa, N., Pramling Samuelsson, I., & Colliver, Y. (2022). Editorial: Early child development in play and education: A cultural–historical paradigm. *Frontiers in Psychology*, *13*, 968473. https://doi.org/10.3389/fpsyg.2022.968473

Woolley, H. (2021). Beyond the fence: Constructed and found spaces for children's outdoor play in natural and human-induced disaster contexts – Lessons from north-east Japan, and Za'atari refugee camp in Jordan. *International Journal of Disaster Risk Reduction*, *56*, 102155. https://doi.org/10.1016/j.ijdrr.2021.102155

Chapter 6

Emotional and social development and traumatic experiences

Introduction

Early childhood educators work to support the optimal development of each child in their care. Their work places children on a pathway to success in school and life. Observers may think academic success rests on strong cognitive skills (*the 3 R's*) alone, but the more we learn about how brains develop, the more we understand cognitive development is deeply interwoven with social and emotional learning (SEL). As children learn about themselves and the world around them, they are developing their ability to learn and thrive in school. Social and emotional skills are developed naturally as young children interact with the people and places in their young lives. Critically, when children face high levels of trauma in early childhood, the natural process of brain development can be delayed or derailed. The brains of children facing relentless stress work doubly hard to strengthen neural connections associated with protective 'fight, flight, or freeze' responses rather than developing parts of the brain associated with self-control, self-confidence, executive functions, and interpersonal relationship. And these are all key school readiness skills as well. The good news is that young, developing brains are incredibly responsive to strong and nurturing early childhood supports, and early care and learning providers who are aware of this reality can help these children to thrive.

Emotional and social competencies

Theories about the relationship between emotion and cognition have been discussed since the times of the ancient Greeks. Various advancements made in technology, societal changes, and the resultant epistemologies and ontological challenges have brought emotional and social skills and sensitivities once again into the realm of everyday practices in childcare, learning environments, and teaching responsibilities. The resurgence of interest in the emotional and social development in the lives of individuals in general and young children and students in particular has been associated with the work of theorists such as Salovey, Mayer, Goleman, and Gardner during the 1980s and 1990s. Developed

DOI: 10.4324/9781003404231-7

and understood from various perspectives, the major focus on social and emotional development at this time was the relationship of social intelligence with the seemingly separate psychological systems of emotion and cognition. In more recent history, these notions had been investigated by theorists such as Thorndike and Cronbach (Cronbach, 1960; Thorndike, 1920; Thorndike & Stein, 1937). However, Salovey and Mayer established a newer, more comprehensive definition for emotions, describing them as interdisciplinary 'organized responses' that arise in response to events that are meaningful for the individual (Mayer et al. 2000, 2004a, 2004b: Salovey & Sluyter, 1997; Salovey & Mayer, 1990). Integrating this notion of emotions with Wechsler's (1958) definition of intelligence, Salovey and Mayer (1990) labelled the set of skills that they hypothesised contributed to the appraisal, regulation, and expression of the emotions of self and others as 'emotional intelligence.' This description was later clarified (Mayer et al., 2004b, p. 197) and the emotional intelligence model developed by these theorists was defined as follows:

> The capacity to reason about emotions, and of emotions to enhance thinking. It includes the abilities to accurately perceive emotions, to access and generate emotions so as to assist thought, to understand emotions and emotional knowledge, and to reflectively regulate emotions so as to promote emotional and intellectual growth.

The influence of Gardner's work on multiples intelligences (Gardner, 1993b) was apparent in the definition developed by Mayer and Salovey as it was closely aligned with how intrapersonal intelligence was defined by Gardner in the original edition of *Frames of Mind* (Gardner, 1983, p. 239). He wrote:

> The core capacity at work here is access to one's own feeling life – one's range of affects or emotions: the capacity instantly to effect discriminations among these feelings and, eventually, to label them, to enmesh them in symbolic codes, to draw upon them as a means of understanding and guiding one's behavior.

Gardner found the notion of intrapersonal intelligence increasingly complex. He redefined it several times in his later writings (1993, 1997, 1999, 2000), consistently emphasising its overall importance in accessing relative strengths in other intelligences and placing these competencies firmly in the realm of cognitive processes. Not only was intrapersonal intelligence reconceptualised as the result of much reflection by the theorist himself, but it also remains the single intelligence that comprises two components: the capacity to access, acknowledge, and identify own emotions, and the aptitude to use this information to succeed in achieving personal goals in various interactions and societal roles. The duality of intrapersonal intelligence remains a unique component in a contentious and hotly debated theory, the misguided practice of which in educational contexts led to criticisms from a number of academic disciplines. Coupled with interpersonal intelligence, this aspect of intrapersonal intelligence is a particularly important component of emotional skills and capacities as appropriate to developmental stages of growth. Mayer et al. (2004a, 2004b) acknowledge, however, that the additional dimension of intrapersonal intelligence, which is the capacity to use the knowledge that is the result of self-awareness effectively in life, is not included in their conceptual model of emotional intelligence. Because of this lack of acknowledgement of the deliberate, conscious use of self-awareness or self-knowledge as a key component of their perceptions of emotional intelligence, model they developed was understood to be heavily influenced by psychologists seeking to broaden thinking about the nature of intelligence, especially those who developed theories of specific multiple intelligences, including Gardner (1983,1993a, 1999a, 1999b), and not as a characteristic which offered the opportunity to improve cognition, psychological health, social integration (Berry, 1997, 2001; Berry et al., 2006), and *salutogenesis* (the capacity of an individual to maintain our physical and mental health in the face of adversity and stress) (Vinje et al., 2017), all of which are critical components for successful integration of families with refugee and asylum-seeker experiences (Ager & Strang, 2008).

Research findings

Early educators we interviewed told us that every aspect of working with young children from families with refugee and migrant experiences is bound up with SEL. Children with these experiences often do not reflect what would be considered 'neurotypical development.' These children may exhibit heightened 'fight, flight, or freeze' responses, and lower levels of self-control and self-management skills. Some may be quick to anger and lash out. Others may be withdrawn. Meeting these children where they are, developmentally, and moving them towards more healthy and adaptive social and emotional and behavioural responses becomes a key part of the work of early childhood education centres working with newly arrived children.

> *Context:* I've worked with children in early childhood centres in a number of American cities. Over the years, I've worked with low-income children and with recently resettled children from families with refugee experiences, many refugees from the Bosnian-Serbian war, with Syrian refugees, and most recently, with refugees from Burma. One thing I've noticed is that developmentally, young refugee children will be all over the map. They will be triggered by things that we wouldn't expect to be an issue.

> … Things are different [with children with refugee experiences], like we may have a child who's 4 or 5 years old and still in diapers, still sucking their thumb. We've had children that age who can't hold a cup, or can't feed

themselves. It makes you realize that you need to change your expectations when you're working with kids who've been through these things. You've got to get rid of all of your expectations, your standard ages and stages of development that we all know: that kids should be able to do this by this time. Those expectations don't apply when you bring in children who have gone through this trauma. You have to ask how those traumatic experiences are affecting their development, social and emotional development, and physical development? How is that going to impact what they do, their behavior, within the classroom? ... One thing that really helps is when they get a little English and start to understand how the school works. You know: line up here, get your lunch, sit down here, and open a milk carton this way. They get that pretty quick, and they could go on off and do it on their own. So the younger kids are going to learn it quickly.

Context: I was working as a preschool teacher with a large public school district (in a large American city on the West Coast) for many years. I worked mostly with immigrant families who were coming from Mexico and Central America. Part of our work as teachers working with young children is to observe children's behaviors, to assess where they are developmentally to evaluate what they are learning. Once we start observing children in their whole complexity, and we start listening and really pay attention to what they say and how they say it, and how they behave and what they do, we might uncover something vital about who children are. And when it comes to children who have gone through these traumatic experiences, it's even more important and more relevant.

...I'll give you as an example, there was a 4 year old little boy named Frank whose family came from El Salvador and he had a lot of behavior issues in the classroom. One day, we were asking children to draw a self-portrait, just a picture of who you think you are. Can you draw a picture of yourself? So he started drawing a sketch of who he believed that he was, And his picture had two figures. One that had half of the face covered. And another with his hands up. And then we asked him: 'can you tell us a little bit about your drawing?' And he said, 'Well, this person is a bandolero. And he said, they are not good people. They shot and killed my grandpa.'

I shared the pictures with Frank's mother. She said, 'Yes, in fact, this story is real. That's the reason why we had to leave El Salvador. My father, Frank's grandfather, was killed. Yes.' And she also shared that when they fled, she had to leave behind Frank's two older sisters. Frank would sometimes say 'I have sisters,' and I didn't believe that he had sisters, because I had never met them. And then it turned out that it was true. He had two sisters, much older than him. His mother said: 'I was risking my life, and I didn't want to risk the lives of my two daughters. So I left them with my mother, with their grandmother.' This all, of course, changed how we viewed little Frank.

His actions that we had labeled as misbehaviors now made sense to us. ... This was a child who was grieving. ... And it changed our perspectives on Frank. And then we were wondering, how many more Franks do we have in the classroom? How many more Franks have we had in all the years that we have in teaching? How many Franks will be coming through these doors?

Unique contexts, global principles

Despite working thousands of miles apart with families from very different parts of the world, these two respondents shared insights that are remarkably aligned. Our first respondent noted educator's expectations of 'neuro-typical development' will be challenged by children who have lived with profound family and home disruption. Children may present with measures of social, emotional, and behavioural development far behind what their chronological age would suggest. Our respondent who has worked extensively with children from families who have fled strife in Latin America notes evaluating and supporting the social and emotional development of displaced children involves patience, and a willingness to understand children in their whole complexity. Only in this way, he suggests, do we come to understand the deep SEL needs these children have.

Our respondents share the view that these SEL delays may be the result of traumatic experiences, and they join with many other respondents in underscoring the need to establish safe and trusting environments for children and families, as a critical threshold for developing adaptive patterns of behavior, and encouraging positive social, emotional, and cognitive development. Care providers are encouraged to move beyond traditional assessments as a sole measure of SEL, recognising these assessments may be mandated by centres and districts. The examples shared suggest providers are on the right track when they are open to additional multi-modal, portfolio-based assessment strategies for assessing children's development and their progress.

Notions of emotional and social learning

The development of the four branch model of emotional intelligence by Mayer et al. (Mayer & Salovey, 1997; Mayer et al., 2004a, 2004b) focuses exclusively on emotions, neglecting some important aspects of emotional and social intelligences that were identified by Gardner as intrapersonal and interpersonal intelligences, most significantly the capacity to use these personal intelligences to understand and guide behaviour in the context of the society in which interactions take place, that is, within one's own cultural and societal environment. Unlike Gardner, Mayer and Salovey (1997) do not explicitly place emphasis on emotional and intellectual growth within social and cultural contexts. It may be taken as given that this is what was assumed as it would be rare for any individual to live without human contact or interaction with society, but to conclude that the maturation process of emotional intelligence is determined by chronological age and not by the quality of the interactions and self-reflective processes that the individual is engaged in appears to be rather narrow-minded and naive. This is especially so in the case of developing these skills with families who have refugee and asylum-seeker experiences, have endured complex traumatic experiences, and who have diverse cultural and social norms which may differ significantly from those espoused by their new homelands.

Other theorists, Goleman (1995a) in particular, did much to bring the notion of emotional intelligence to the notice of the general public, attracting popular acclaim and acceptance. Despite its public appeal, Goleman's work on emotional intelligence (1995) appears also to have attracted a significant degree of academic criticism. Mayer et al. (2000, p. 102) comment that 'at first it was presented as a journalistic account of our own theory,' despite the resultant publication containing significant differences to their work, most notably the absence of any attempt to develop or explore any relationship between emotion or cognition: a critical focus of the work of Mayer et al. (2004a, 2004b). Another issue centres around Goleman's (1995) reluctance to decide on a definition for emotional intelligence. While Gardner may have developed and refined the definition of intrapersonal intelligence (Gardner, 1983, 1993a, 1999a, 1999b; Moran & Gardner, 2007) over a period of many years and as the result of reflection, Goleman's definition 'snowballed' within the text until the traits included in his final definition were described by Mayer et al. as it 'encompasses the entire model of how one operates in the world' (Mayer et al., 2000, pp. 101–102). Gardner (Noble & Grant, 1997, pp. 24–26) also appears to have some problems with Goleman's model of emotional intelligence which is more significant for those with diverse cultures, beliefs, value systems, and ways of doing and knowing.

> Interpersonal and intrapersonal intelligences add up to Dan Goleman's emotional intelligence. But I think he goes on to talk about other things like having a certain stance on life. ... My major quibble with his book is that he kind of collapses description and prescription ... I think that Dan wants people to be a certain way.
>
> (Noble & Grant, 1997 p 24–26)

This comment by Gardner which reflects his problems with Goleman's (1995) model of emotional intelligence is particularly pertinent for those who are considered different to the mainstream society. Gardner notes that this model goes beyond the boundaries of Gardner's own understanding of the personal intelligences, which are part of a theory of cognition. It is possible that the prescriptive nature of Goleman's work actually places boundaries on the potential of individuals to develop these intelligences and that it may even promote a type of homogeneity that is contrary to Gardner's emphasis on the need to find personal meaning and understanding in life. More significant, however, for families with refugee and asylum-seeker experiences and their carers and teachers is that while Gardner's (1983, 1993a, 1999a, 1999b) intrapersonal intelligence domain requires individuals to express this self-knowledge as the skills of executive function, Goleman's (1995) theory of emotional intelligence appears to require individuals to conform to a particular perspective of life that is the most socially acceptable, aligning it more closely with notions of acculturation and assimilation, and not with authentic integration (Ager & Strang, 2008; Berry, 1997, 2001; Berry et al., 2006).

Research findings

Our respondents spoke of the many pathways and environments young children must navigate before they reached childcare and early learning settings in their new homes. In turn, these contexts and experiences shaped children's development and, in large part, may explain both the wide range of abilities and developmental levels newly arriving children exhibit, and they have implications for newcomers' interpersonal skills and – by extension – their readiness to engage in a positive way with teachers and peers.

> *Context:* I worked with children from African refugee families (to Australia). While the adults were doing life skills training; we would take the children to the local church and run a playgroup. … We would collect these children, walk around to the church, and set up a playgroup. It was very fast-track learning. In my experience, children's violent behavior may be a direct reflection of their parents' actions. Many of the parents that we see may have grown up in refugee camps and may have met their spouses and married, and had their children in the camps. And camp life for many refugees was characterized by high levels of violence.

> A lot of the parents, when they first came, were very hostile with each other, and they told me there were incidences of them throwing chairs at each other and things like that. It was a bit of a rocky start, and we had to develop all of these teaching strategies to respond to that. We were a lot different to what mainstream early childhood education would be. We had to do a lot of active–passive work constantly. We couldn't have blocks and things like that because the children would throw the blocks at each other. So we did something like bubbles and singing and dancing, running games and just lots of active stuff with them.

> We also learned that some children will replicate social relationships and orderings that they might have experienced in refugee camps. We had one boy, who was newly arrived, and he seemed to be the group leader. It was explained to me that it was culturally appropriate for them to have a bit of a leader, and they would all do the same thing as him. So if he fell onto the

ground, they would all fall to the ground. So it was quite interesting, I've never experienced that before. … [W]e sort of realized that the group of boys needed the stability and leadership this boy represented. Once we got him on board, things were a lot better. … So the key is that you've got to build that trusting relationship with them in order to understand, because otherwise parents don't tend to come forward, particularly for some cultures like the Vietnamese families, who, you know, don't question a teacher, and won't even complain about anything. So yeah, there are different patterns of development and different cultures, depending on what country that the child comes from (Tammy, Australia).

Context: I have tried to retire a number of times, most recently from a professorship at the University working with students who want to go into early childhood education. My current work is with a social service agency that runs a preschool and does home visiting for at-risk children and families (in a large midwestern American city). In that role, I see many recently arrived children, including children from families with refugee experiences.

The trauma that many of these children have experienced is real, complex and multi-faceted. Their behavior will tell you what you know, and it will help you understand how to react. At its heart, what they need is unconditional safety and love. Failure is heart-breaking for them. They aren't prepared to handle it. They simply cannot handle any expectations that they are not ready for. Little successes count for so much. They are not ready for strings of directions. Just one or two step directions.

We as teachers have so many opportunities to disrupt anti-social behavior, and to soothe these children, and help them calm down. I remember a little boy named King, who had experienced some awful things. When he was angry and upset, he would hit the fish tank. He was so angry he wanted to hurt the fish. I thought he might break the glass. I knew that King loved the Alicia Keyes song 'The Girl is On Fire,' and I would have it cued up on my phone. When he would get so angry and run at the fish tank I would quickly press play on my phone, and the song would start. It was just enough to catch him off guard, just for a second, but it was enough of a disruption to let him catch himself. And he would turn to me and say 'I'm doing it, aren't I?' And we both would laugh. That small disruption was just enough to allow him to add a breath before he would respond.

Unique contexts, global principles

Early childhood brain development involves the development of a child's ability to both interact with the world around her and also to develop an understanding of, and an ability to manage, herself. Our Australian respondent shared an anecdote about group dynamics observed among children who had spent time in refugee camps, where they had developed a strong reliance on a group of peers. Rather than attack the gang-like nature of the peer group directly, our respondent and her colleagues worked with the group's leader to leverage the feelings of safety and belonging the group provided. Meanwhile, our American respondent created an innovative 'disruption' that allowed her to help one young student learn to pause before lashing out from a position of anger and frustration.

In both of these instances, our respondents shared the importance of helping children learn to manage both the internal and external manifestations of feelings and emotions that could easily be overwhelming for small children, and help them develop the skills they will need to respond to these feelings in developmentally appropriate ways (for example, learning to resolve conflict through language rather than through physical violence). Learning how to understand, and redirect, maladaptive behaviour in early childhood is a difficult part of the role of early childhood educators, and it is a particularly vital part of their role when they are providing care for children with refugee experiences.

Emotional and social learning: the challenges

There are several challenges that may be presented by babies, toddlers, and young children with refugee and asylum-seeker experiences when carers and educators endeavour to promote emotional and social knowledge for these cohorts. Firstly, the adverse impact of the build-up of cortisol created by traumatic events that impair effective cognitive functioning and development (Alayarian, 2018; Chen et al., 2009; Montgomery, 2010; Scheeringa & Zeanah, 2001; Teicher et al., 2003; Weiland et al., 2014; Weiss, 2007) is also understood to influence the achievement of emotional and social developmental milestones negatively. This may be because of the memories that create and re-create negative emotions as memories, nightmares, fears for future events, interpretations or anticipations of ongoing interactions as traumatic (Fazel & Stein, 2002; Sapmaz et al., 2017; Speidel et al., 2021). It may also be because cognition and emotion are no longer considered to be neurologically separate entities in the brain. Pessoa (2008, p. 148) writes:

> In the past two decades, several researchers have emphasized that emotion and cognition systems interact in important ways. Here, I will argue that there are no truly separate systems for emotion and cognition because complex cognitive–emotional behaviour emerges from the rich, dynamic interactions between brain networks. Indeed, I propose that emotion and cognition not only strongly interact in the brain, but that they are often integrated so that they jointly contribute to behaviour. Moreover, I propose that emotion and cognition are only minimally decomposable in the brain, and that the neural basis of emotion and cognition should be viewed as strongly non modular.

Studies of this interrelationship of cognition and emotion have been signifi-cantly facilitated by the development of functional MRI scanning (fMRI), a device that facilitated the development of the Broaden and Build model de-signed by Fredrickson (2000, 2001, 2003), to illustrate the importance of positive emotion in facilitating cognition, especially in novel situations and problem-solving. A more significant impact of early trauma for the successful emotional and social learning of very young children with refugee and asylum-seeker experiences is that they may have developed survival patterns and alter-native ways of coping that predispose them to severe psychological distress and disorders. Teicher et al. (2003, p. 39) explain:

> In short, we propose that the brain goes through a sensitive period in post-natal life in which exposure to high levels of stress hormones select for an alternative pathway of development that occurs through a cascade of neu-robiological effects.
>
> That is, exposure to significant stressors during a sensitive developmen-tal period causes the brain to develop along a stress-responsive pathway. Further, we hypothesize that exposure to corticosteroids is a crucial fac-tor in organizing the brain to develop in this manner....In our hypothesis, postnatal neglect or other maltreatment serves to elicit a cascade of stress responses that organizes the brain to develop along a specific pathway se-lected to facilitate reproductive success and survival in a world of depriva-tion and strife. This pathway, however, is costly as it is associated with an increased risk of developing serious medical and psychiatric disorders and is unnecessary and maladaptive in a more benign environment.

In their review and evaluation of early childhood interventions, policies, and practices designed to support children who have experienced disadvan-tageous circumstances leading to 'at risk' determinations being made about their developmental processes, Shonkoff and Fisher (2013) discussed the change of focus in preschool practices during and after the 1990s. It was dur-ing these decades that the attention was redirected from preparing preschool-ers for school in academic domains such as the developing of language and pre-arithmetic and pre-reading skills to the importance of preparing them with skills in SEL, leaning heavily towards play-based interactions and activi-ties that reflect their individual interests and the early development of the capacities of executive skills such as working memory, flexible thinking, and initiating tasks. A major contribution of their work was the critical nature of the learning environment. It was considered imperative to build capacity in the caregivers, not only in formal educational settings but also for the parents and other caregivers. They termed this a two-generational approach, under-standing that among all the other circumstances that may have caused children to be at risk, poverty was a major contributor, a condition not unknown to many families with refugee and asylum-seeker experiences. Learning and living environments which facilitate the identification and exploration of children's interests have the potential to develop the interpersonal intelligence Gardner proposes and both facets of the intrapersonal interpersonal intelligence he values as critical to well-being and development. These recommendations place much responsibility on early childhood carers and teachers' own capacities to engage in professional practices of care which is educative and supportive of both the children in their care and their parents. This may prove to be very demanding. It may take many repetitions of positive experiences on specific parts of the brain to mediate stress responses or to stimulate those areas not sufficiently developed by neglect, especially in cases of exposure to violence (Twardosz & Lutzker, 2010). There is the question of who determines the nature of tasks, activities, and interactions given the diverse understandings of childhood and the value of play that are held by disparate communities based on specific ontologies and epistemologies. Additionally, the cultural and social dimensions of desirable and acceptable social and emotional understanding and behaviour influence interpretations of emotional and social behaviours, which are underpinned, in each community, by the values and thought patterns which are deeply held, unconscious, subjective, implicitly learned, and difficult to change (Hall, 1976).

Research findings

Our respondents were consistent that SEL is a necessary component of early childhood development and, without it, cognitive development simply cannot occur. In turn, school readiness rests on a foundation of social and emotional, as well as cognitive, learning. Many factors can undermine neuro-typical social emotional learning, locking brains in a 'flight, fight, or freeze' mode. Often grouped under the heading Adverse Childhood Experiences (ACEs), these factors include ongoing exposure to poverty, violence, and neglect. We spoke with a head teacher in England and a principal in Australia who shared perspectives on the power of interventions to help guide children towards a positive developmental pathway.

> *Context:* I'm the executive head teacher at a school for children from disadvantaged communities (in a large city in the north of England). This is a community that faces a huge number of challenges and is very diverse. We've got young people and families from all over the world.
>
> I would say that time and trust are powerful tools in the early educator's toolkit, but then, alongside that, there may be a need for these children to have some therapeutic counseling, because some of these kids have been through a lot. Some families have been through a lot to get here. So we have a counsellor. We are fortunate to have support from a national charity

which provides the resources which allow us to have four counsellors working with the children. All of the children in school can drop in. They kind of just book in a slot. But then we have, at any one time we have 16 children having intensive therapeutic work done.

Context: I'm the principal at a public school in the western suburbs of [a large Australian city] with a preschool. I've been the principal there for more than five years. In my experience, I would say the first need for these children and their families is to feel safe and to trust the center and the staff. That is the foundation for creating a positive environment that allows for learning (for both the children and their parents)

We believe that safety and security must come first in order to prepare these families and children for the transition into kindergarten. Once the children are feeling safe, and the child and their family are comfortable with us and feel secure, then we can start to worry about the curriculum and all the additional extra things that go on. So ensuring that there are positive relationships developing between the child and their peers and fellow students, and between the child and their teacher, is critical. Learning will not happen unless there's a safe and trusting relationship between the student and the teacher and between the student and their peers.

Unique contexts, global principles

Our lead teacher from the north of England spoke of the foundational need to create environments where children feel safe and secure, and she noted the importance of time and trust in building that environment. But she also cautioned that creating a welcoming environment may not be enough in and of itself. Newly arrived students with traumatic backgrounds may need more direct and intensive therapeutic interventions. This centre's counselling staff is enviably robust, thanks to philanthropic funding. The centre serves children in a disadvantaged community with high levels of violence and family disruption. Rather than mark the end of their traumatic experiences, relocation to these neighbourhoods can create new traumatic experiences for children and families. Based on her experience in an Australian childcare centre, our second respondent underscored the foundational importance of safety and trust, which make it possible to build a platform of social and emotional security and, in turn, make it possible to turn to curriculum and other dimensions of cognitive development. Traditional learning, she notes, will not happen unless the foundation of safety and security is in place.

Learning involves risk-taking, and traumatised children are incredibly sensitive to risk and to the possibility of danger and failure. In other words, SEL are not simply about self-regulation, but they also are keys that help unlock the trove of psychological safety that is needed to allow children to take risks and venture beyond their comfort zone to learn and develop. Early childhood educators working with vulnerable groups of children must strike a delicate balance. On the one hand, they are working to establish an environment where children feel safe and secure. On the other hand, and when the time is right, educators are gently nudging children in the direction of exploration: through play, and through guided investigation of the world around them. Early childhood classroom environments can be structured to encourage safe exploration (e.g. through centres that encourage children's autonomy, a rich selection of daily activities that gently challenge children with different modes of learning, and various levels of structured and unstructured playtime, as well as provide opportunities for both group engagement and individual quests). Observation and flexibility are two of the most important tools in the early educator's toolkit, as he or she works to understand each child's current zone of proximal development and capacity to venture forward on their own learning journey, and to adjust the learning environment accordingly.

Conclusion

Encouraging the development of emotional and social learning is a fundamental component of effective early childhood education and intervention efforts. As such, it is at the heart of the work of early educators. Pillars of school readiness include cognitive skills, including language and early-literacy and numeracy development. No less important are other pillars of readiness that are more closely linked to emotional and social skills. Kindergarten teachers talk about self-confidence and self-control for example. Our respondents shared ways SEL may be delayed for children from families with refugee experiences, who may present with measures of development far behind their neuro-typical peers. Our respondents attribute these delays to trauma and adversity in early childhood, and are of one mind in their belief that social and emotional delays must be addressed before children will be ready to venture down a more traditional curricular path. This reality poses special challenges for children from families with refugee experiences. As the stories shared in this chapter indicate, these children may present with social and emotional delays, and with behavioural patterns that must be addressed before it is possible to turn to traditional academic skills. Our stories highlight children acting out in ways that resonate with the idea of 'fight, flight, or freeze.' Frank, who carried the trauma of violence in his family's past into his conception of himself, and King, who channelled his fury into punching the fishtank, both were learning how to deal with fear and rage, and express their feelings in appropriate ways. Both of these stories also indicate ways providers can disrupt maladaptive behaviors: for Frank, his drawing became an opportunity to begin a conversation with his mother about how best to help her to support his development. For King, a beloved song became a cue to pause before acting, and an opportunity to allow his brain to check his own feelings and find an appropriate response before lashing out.

References

Ager, A., & Strang, A. (2008). Understanding integration: A conceptual framework. *Journal of Refugee Studies, 21*(2), 166–191. https://doi.org/10.1093/jrs/fen016

Alayarian, A. (2018). *Handbook of working with children, trauma, and resilience: An intercultural psychoanalytic view.* Taylor & Francis Group.

Berry, J. (1997). Immigration, acculturation, and adaptation. *Applied Psychology: An International Review, 46*(1), 5–68.

Berry, J. (2001). A psychology of immigration. *Journal of Social Issues, 7*(3), 615–631.

Berry, J., Phinney, J., Sam, D., & Vedder, P. (2006). Immigrant youth: Acculturation, identity, and adaptation. *Applied Psychology: An International Review, 55*(3), 303–332.

Chen, E., Cohen, S., & Miller, G. E. (2009). How low socioeconomic status affects 2-year hormonal trajectories in children. *Psychological Science, 21*(1), 31–37. https://doi.org/10.1177/0956797609355566

Cronbach, L. (1960). *Essentials of psychological testing* (2nd ed.). Harper and Row.

Fazel, M., & Stein, A. (2002). The mental health of refugee children. *Archives of Disease in Childhood, 87*(5), 366–370.

Fredrickson, B. (2000). Cultivating positive emotions to optimize health and well-being. *Prevention and Treatment, 3.*

Fredrickson, B. (2001). The role of positive emotions in positive psychology. *American Psychologist, 56*(3), 218–226.

Fredrickson, B. L. (2003). The value of positive emotions: The emerging science of positive psychology is coming to understand why it's good to feel good. *American Scientist, 91*(4), 330–335.

Gardner, H. (1983). *Frames of mind: The theory of multiple intelligences.* Basic Books.

Gardner, H. (1993a). *Frames of mind* (Tenth Anniversary ed.). Basic Books.

Gardner, H. (1999a). *The disciplined mind: What all students should understand.* Simon and Shuster.

Gardner, H. (1999b). *Intelligence reframed: Multiple intelligences for the 21st century.* Basic Books.

Goleman, D. (2007). Social intelligence. Arrow Books.

Hall, E. (1976). *Beyond culture.* Knopf Doubleday Publishing Group.

Mayer, J., & Salovey, P (1997). What is emotional intelligence? In P. Salovey & D. Sluyter (Eds.), *Emotional development and emotional intelligence.* Basic Books.

Mayer, J., Salovey, P, & Caruso, D. (2000). Emotional intelligence as zeitgeist, as personality, and as a mental ability. In R. Bar-On, & J. Parker (Eds.), *The handbook of emotional intelligence.* Jossey- Bass.

Mayer, J., Savoley, P, & Caruso, D. (2004a). A further consideration of the issues of emotional intelligence. *Psychological Inquiry, 15*(3), 249–255.

Mayer, J., Savoley, P, & Caruso, D. (2004b). Emotional intelligence: Theory, findings and implications. *Psychological Inquiry*, *15*(3), 197–215.

Montgomery, E. (2010). Trauma and resilience in young refugees: A 9-year follow-up study. *Development and Psychopathology*, *22*(2), 477–489. https://doi.org/10.1017/S0954579410000180

Moran, S., & Gardner, H. (2018). Hill, skill, and will: executive function from a multiple-intelligences perspective. In Executive function in education: From theory to practice, 2nd ed. (pp. 25-56). The Guilford Press.

Noble, T. (2004). Integrating the Revised Bloom's Taxonomy with Multiple Intelligences: A Planning Tool for Curriculum Differentiation. Teachers College Record, *106*(1), 193-211. https://doi.org/10.1111/j.1467-9620.2004.00328.x

Pessoa, L. (2008). On the relationship between emotion and cognition. *Nature Reviews: Neuroscience*, *9*(2), 148–158. https://doi.org/10.1038/nrn2317

Salovey, P., & Mayer, J. (1990). *Emotional Intelligence*. Baywood Publishing Co. Ltd.

Salovey, P., & Sluyter, D. (Eds.). (1997). *Emotional development and emotional intelligence*. Basic Books.

Sapmaz, Ş. Y., Tanrıverdi, B. U., Öztürk, M., Gözaçanlar, Ö., Ülker, G. Y., & Özkan, Y. (2017). Immigration-related mental health disorders in refugees 5–18 years old living in Turkey. *Neuropsychiatric Disease and Treatment*, *13*, 2813–2821.

Scheeringa, M. S., & Zeanah, C. H. (2001). A relational perspective on PTSD in early childhood. *Journal of Traumatic Stress*, *14*(4), 799–815. https://doi.org/10.1023/a:1013002507972

Shonkoff, J. P., & Fisher, P. A. (2013). Rethinking evidence-based practice and two-generation programs to create the future of early childhood policy. *Development and Psychopathology*, *25*(4pt2), 1635–1653.

Speidel, R., Galarneau, E., Elsayed, D., Mahhouk, S., Filippelli, J., Colasante, T., & Malti, T. (2021). Refugee children's social–emotional capacities: Links to mental health upon resettlement and buffering effects on pre-migratory adversity. *International Journal of Environmental Research and Public Health*, *18*(22), 12180. https://doi.org/10.3390/ijerph182212180

Teicher, M. H., Andersen, S. L., Polcari, A., Anderson, C. M., Navalta, C. P., & Kim, D. M. (2003). The neurobiological consequences of early stress and childhood maltreatment. *Neuroscience & Biobehavioral Reviews*, *27*(1–2), 33–44.

Thorndike, E. (1920). Intelligence and its uses. *Harper's Magazine*, *140*, 227–235.

Thorndike, E., & Stein, S. (1937). An evaluation of the attempts to measure social intelligence. *Psychological Bulletin*, *34*, 275–284.

Twardosz, S., & Lutzker, J. R. (2010). Child maltreatment and the developing brain: A review of neuroscience perspectives. *Aggression and Violent Behavior*, *15*(1), 59–68.

Vinje, H. F., Langeland, E., & Bull, T. (2017). Aaron Antonovsky's development of salutogenesis, 1979 to 1994. In M. B. Mittelmark et al. *The Handbook of Salutogenesis* (pp. 25–40). Springer International Publishing. https://doi.org/10.1007/978-3-319-04600-6_4

Wechsler, D. (1958). *The measurement and appraisal of adult intelligence*. Williams & Wilkins.

44

Weiland, C., Barata, M. C., & Yoshikawa, H. (2014). The co-occurring development of executive function skills and receptive vocabulary in preschool-aged children: A look at the direction of the developmental pathways. *Infant and Child Development*, *23*(1), 4–21. https://doi.org/10.1002/icd.1829

Weiss, S. J. (2007). Neurobiological alterations associated with traumatic stress. *Perspectives in Psychiatric Care*, *43*(3), 114–122. https://doi.org/10.1111/j.1744-6163.2007.00120.x

Chapter 7

Intergenerational trauma and trauma in communities

Introduction

Violence, loss, and displacement can produce immediate impacts on the well-being of individuals and leave them dealing with the resulting trauma for years. Through decades of research, we know trauma is passed from parents to children and can negatively alter the way our youngest children view the world, engage with peers, focus in classrooms, and respond to challenges. Intergenerational trauma makes the work of those who support families with refugee backgrounds more complex. This chapter offers an understanding of intergenerational trauma, a look at how communities in host countries often contribute to this trauma, and the roles caregivers can play in addressing intergenerational trauma.

Cultural perspectives of trauma

As a preface to the discussion of intergenerational trauma, it may be informative to gain some broad insight into the different ways in which mental health is viewed in diverse cultures. As a review of the literature (Gopalkrishnan, 2018) indicates, the ways in which mind and body are perceived to be in relationship with each other varies from group to group. Western notions of mental healthcare have proved to be problematic in several aspects when applied in the context of non-Western individuals. Hernandez et al. (2009, p. 1047) suggest that 'culture influences what gets defined as a problem, how the problem is understood and which solutions to the problem are acceptable.' Further to this, Gopalkrishnan (2018, p. 2) documents the framework of five key components developed by Hechanova et al. (2020) that must be considered when considering the cultural complications of applying Western approaches and strategies to individuals with refugee experiences who hold varied beliefs about mental health considerations such as the impacts of trauma and Western notions of intergenerational trauma. He notes that Hechanova et al. (2020) place emotion expression as the first component. This is the case where cultures belief is that lack of balance in emotional expression can lead

DOI: 10.4324/9781003404231-8

to symptoms and to disease itself. It may also be that actually speaking about the experiences which are painful will lead to even further pain. Consequently, individuals with refugee experiences from certain communities in Southeast Asia and Africa may not wish to participate in therapies which involve discussing these events or how they feel about the impact of them.

The second component is shame. Research indicates that Asian refugee or asylum seekers may frequently experience shame because of the role that family and community play in their lives and this may bring dishonour to their extended families. The third component is power distance. Identified as one dimension of culture by Hofstede (2011), this reflects the lack of equal relationship between patient and therapist as observed in some, predominantly Asian, cultures. This lack of autonomy may lead individuals to resist therapeutic treatments, prolonging the chemical imbalances created by their responses and inhibiting rebalancing of the hormones that support healthy development, healing, and positivity. The fourth is discussed as the nature of collectivist societies, where being part of a supportive community acts as a positive element in the development of resilience and coping strategies. However, this may also impact as gendered differences as many of such cultures are hierarchical with strict codes for males and definitions of masculinity. The final component discussed is religion and spirituality in general. The ways in which these belief systems impact on how suffering and disease is understood and explained. Hechanova et al. (2020) observe that these cultural factors impact on several aspects of mental health support and provision services as they can determine how individuals engage with interventions and therapy, how satisfied they are with the treatment, and, consequently, the outcomes of the therapy.

Tribe (2002, p. 242) lists the issues that individuals with refugee experiences may suffer. These include war, human rights abuses, persecution on grounds of politics, religion, gender, or ethnicity, loss of country, culture, family, profession, language, friends, and plans for future. Additionally, there are issues that may be experienced in countries of asylum or resettlement. These include multiple change, psychological and practical adjustment, uncertain futures, traumatic life events, hardship, racism, stereotyping by host community, and unknown cultural traditions. When faced with the enormity of the implications of displacement and subsequent events, it is not difficult to understand the potential for intergenerational trauma to exist and persist in many forms, both psychically and psychologically.

Understanding intergenerational trauma

Quality care is critical to supporting children to overcome these difficulties. However, many parents and caregivers are themselves in need of support and intervention as the result of trauma. As a result, those who care for babies, toddlers, and children in the contexts of early childcare and schooling have the additional task of seeking to understand and address the impacts of not only the various types and disadvantages of childhood traumas, but also of offering additional, appropriate support to the parents and caregivers. It is possible, and likely to be probable, that the offspring of traumatised parents and caregivers develop the behaviours, symptoms, and signs of trauma themselves, irrespective of their lack of first-hand experiences. Incidents of intergenerational trauma are well researched and documented (Bowers & Yehuda, 2016; Masten, 2014; Masten, 2016; Masten & Shaffer, 2006; Menzies, 2010; Raphael et al., 1998; Schechter, 2010). This notion of intergenerational trauma began with anecdotal evidence of the children of Holocaust survivors and continued to be investigated in terms of social and behavioural theory. This perspective offered the view that behaviours triggered or modified by the traumatic experiences of the parents were adopted by their children. Bowers and Yehuda (2016, p. 232) note that these may be physical, behavioural, and cognitive traits that are modelled by traumatised parents.

Additionally, they propose that trauma may also be transmitted biologically, via the reproductive cells of traumatised parents, altering the chemical balances *in utero* and impacting on early postnatal care. Mothers who experience trauma during pregnancy were also found to be affected. The maternal stress in the final trimester was found to have the most impact on the infant's health, potentially leading to physical and emotional problems as they grew older. Van Ee et al. (2012) found that the levels of mothers' postnatal trauma was directly correlated with degrees of psychological and social impairment in their infants. Further studies explored the notion of transmitted trauma, including the impact of trauma on the children of adolescent mothers (Stargel & Easterbrooks, 2020) and the impact of maternal adverse childhood experiences on the development of their offspring (Sun et al., 2017). While there may be something of a tendency to think that babies and young children of parents with refugee and asylum-seeker experiences who are born in the new homelands will have no symptoms or experiences of trauma, that may be a rather naive perspective, given the degree of research attention that intergenerational trauma has gained in the past few decades. Much of this new information has been gathered in relation to entire communities, not simply individual cases, who have a history of traumatic experiences throughout generations, resulting in widespread community characteristics in addition to personal distress.

Research findings

Recognising the signs and then supporting young children who are suffering the effects of intergenerational trauma can be challenging. We interviewed an Australian day care provider and an Australian day care director who shared anecdotes of parents and young children struggling with the consequences of forced displacement, loss, and resettlement.

Context: I've been working for more than five years now. We had many children from Syria and many refugees from Africa and Iraq who were coming to [mid-sized Australian city]. We started with more than 20 kids. We are a very small centre. I call it unique and special because it is really special. It doesn't have the facilities of other normal childcares, like outdoor and lots of facilities that the children can use to learn and grow. But in the sense of these children's needs, they need special care and learning. This centre is really small and serves all ages from 6 months to under five years. They stay there together in one room.

The idea of having your child in out-of-home care is a new experience. Because can you imagine mothers gave birth to their children during the time that they were in refugee camps, and they've been staying there for so long, many years. They don't know the school environment, early education environment. All these things are new for them. They are experiencing in Australia for the very first time. Some children have even not been left with other family members.

Context: We have a combination of refugee families and anyone who's migrated to Australia. So, we're right in this city centre, a very small childcare centre because we are in a commercial building, specifically two large rooms, and my office. Our capacity is a bit limited because of the location of the centre. So, we have space for eight babies in the baby room, and then we have the preschool between 2 to 5 years age group. So, parents have the option of keeping their child until preschool age. It's very dynamic; we have all kinds of different situations here. The youngest we've had is 7 months, and the oldest is five and a half.

We were having behavioural problems with the children. This is what happened with this family fleeing their home country. They went to a third country where these two children were born. They lived there for four years in a refugee camp; then, they moved to Australia. So, the two children were born in trauma; intergenerational trauma was happening. I checked in their forms that their emergency contact was the father's cousin. I called him, and his English was pretty good, and you know, a very nice young man. I just said that we're having some issues with the children adjusting. Do you mind coming in to translate? Then he was telling the family in their language, 'You'll be fine. You're all going to be okay.' So, this was on a Friday; I guess they had the weekend to cool down and talk to the cousin, and I think they didn't even tell him anything about what was happening. That's also another stigma. Because you don't want to tell people that, you know, you're having these issues.

Unique contexts, global principles

It is understandable that people who have been forcibly displaced live with persistent worry and uncertainty. Losing your home, then finding yourself and your young family in an unsafe refugee camp for years, before migrating to a foreign country, must produce a level of anxiety in people that is palpable. For young children whose parents are their entire world, this constant exposure to their stress can take a toll. Our first respondent shared an experience that was all too common in our research findings, namely families unable to separate at the preschool door. In this case, a mother who gave birth to her children in a refugee camp and raised them in constant worry and uncertainty was unwilling to lose sight of them. Our participant was clear that her centre allows parents to sit in the room with their children until they are comfortable with the situation. Our second interviewee was attempting to address behaviour issues with children who also had known life only in a refugee camp. In this case, the centre director worked with an extended family member to address the concerns, but she also surmised the family kept their struggles confidential. This participant highlighted the fact that along with the trauma of forced migration, for people with refugee backgrounds, there is also a need to convey some level of control to the outside world.

While many newly arrived children may not have directly experienced violence and loss, they may have spent their entire lives with loving parents who have been processing their own lived horrors and grief. The caustic effects of this trauma shape individuals and alter their behaviour. Children, closely attuned to the world, feel their parents' anxiety and often have their own challenges as a result. For early educators attempting to address social, academic, or emotional issues with these children, it is helpful to understand the lived experiences of the families and the current lives of parents and grandparents who are serving as caregivers. While it might be rational to assume time will help young children adapt, for those who are returning home each afternoon to family members in distress, they are constantly facing the effects of trauma and will continue to bring those challenges into their learning environments. As our research participants demonstrated, educators can be helpful by not forcing families to separate and by reaching out to extended community networks to support families who are struggling. Further, educators need to be cognisant of the fact that newly arrived families could be concerned with appearing to have things under control for many reasons, including, but not limited to, they have had little control over their lives for many years, they don't want to appear to be failing in their host country, and that they are attempting to model some level of stability for their young children.

Trauma in communities

Intergenerational trauma is a vicious cycle. Exposure to intergenerational trauma renders healing more difficult in a number of ways. Frequently created by displacement and disempowerment, as with refugee and asylum-seeker communities, it erodes the cultural and social values which bind people together as societies and enable the development of both common and personal identity (Buonagurio, 2020; O'Brien & Hoffstaedter, 2020). This is elaborated on by studies into indigenous communities who remain as refugees in their own lands (Bombay et al., 2009; McCarty & Wyman, 2009; Menzies, 2010). It is also given credence by the experiences of minority groups such as those subjected to genocide, such as the Rohingya people of Myanmar and the Tutsi tribe in Rwanda (O'Brien & Hoffstaedter, 2020; Uvin, 2003), from which many of the survivors became refugees. Given the importance placed by Berry and his colleagues (Berry, 1997, 2001; Berry et al., 2006) on the psychological and social benefits of balancing and dignifying both the cultural mores of the first homeland and those of the new homeland, impacts of intergenerational trauma on entire communities present substantial problems for those seeking to integrate into new environments where perspectives and world views are significantly different to those from which they have fled. Intergenerational trauma is considered to be a predictor of lifelong mental health concerns, including psychiatric issues and depression, across a range of resettlement environments (Alhassen et al., 2021; Ellis et al., 2008; Henley & Robinson, 2011; Lustig et al., 2004; Montgomery, 2011). This may occur *in utero* as genes behave differently in response to environments and behaviours and which impact on the developing foetus (Dozio et al., 2020) or as the mimicking of social and individual behaviours displayed by the parents or other members of the traumatised community (Bowers & Yehuda, 2016). Toxic stress or trauma transmitted in childhood may last well into adolescence (Montgomery, 2010) and adulthood, rendering individuals unable to successfully complete everyday tasks, including adequately caring for themselves and their children (Gronski et al., 2013; Yehuda & Lehrner, 2018). It may easily be that much intergenerational trauma is created during the journey of resettlement, in the process of integration (or, in some contexts acculturation) and after resettlement itself (Ager & Strang, 2008; Alemi & Stempel, 2018; Baak, 2019; Beiser & Hou, 2016; Brooks & Watson, 2019; Carlile, 2012; Davidson et al., 2004; Goodnow, 2014; Migliarini, 2017; Napolitano et al., 2018; White et al., 2017). This may not only perpetuate the cycle of intergenerational stress, but also increase its impact as the tensions of raising children in a culture which has different traditions and legislative boundaries to that which are familiar to the resettled community and social groups, have to be continually, and not always successfully negotiated (Bornstein, 2012; Deng & Marlowe, 2013; Lewig et al., 2010). In this way, entire communities have traditional child-raising practices challenged and redefined, creating some loss of communal identity and raising the levels of disempowerment and subsequent stress, creating intergenerational differences and disparities, especially in members of collectivist societies (Hofstede, 2001, 2011), whose perceptions of gendered and familial roles are focused on communal well-being, heritage, well-defined responsibilities, and looking backwards to traditional wisdoms (Hofstede et al., 2010).

Research findings

Fleeing violence, witnessing more violence on the journey to your host country and then settling in a dangerous community is often the trajectory of families with refugee experiences. We spoke with a childcare centre director in Australia and one in the United States who offered compelling insights about the caustic effects of ongoing trauma.

> *Context:* I have been engaged in supporting families for 20 years. We partner with childcare centres. We try to match the cultures of our educators and their languages with those of the families we support. So, for example, in a suburb here there is a really huge migrant and refugee population, we make sure that we have educators who speak their languages because most of these families will have very little English or absolutely no English.

> Another point I put down was that our brains have cognitive maps that guide us through our daily lives. So, we need to be mindful that when our families arrive at our services, some may leave the refugee camps. I had one man who told me, 'I had arrived at a refugee camp, and I was there for 15 years and married my wife. We've got two babies, and now we are in Australia.' So, this father, for example, has most of his life that he's spending in a refugee camp. So, trying to understand that when you have families who arrived from these, you know the context, their way of thinking, might be about survival. Just making sure you protect your family because a couple of fathers who arrived from refugee camps told me, 'I had to carry a gun because if you don't have a gun, you might not be alive because of all the different gangs in refugee camps. where there are 10,000 people.'

> *Context:* I directed a non-profit early childhood centre birth through school age for over 20 years in a large US city. I've always worked with low-income families, so the average income of the family served would be under the poverty level. We were fortunate, we had a full-time social worker on staff who was very helpful and who worked to help all our families. Because of the income levels and everyone needed access to jobs, training, and support for childcare payments, we would use a local language institute when language was a barrier. Often it was their older kids who would come in to help us.

> Many kids experience violence in their homes, not from refugee families, but because of the circumstances. The neighbourhood in which I still live is relatively high crime, and the area where the childcare centre was focused was also high crime.

Unique contexts, global principles

Violence and the ongoing threat of violence influences how people behave. Our Australian childcare director offered insight about a parent who spent most of his life living in fear of violence in a refugee camp. This director's contention that those years of worry have created a 'cognitive map' in the father's head is a thoughtful way of understanding how experience shapes thinking and actions. This father likely takes a defensive posture with his interactions and is mindful of protecting his family from real and perceived threats. This defensive posture has undoubtedly influenced the way his children perceive him. Our American director highlighted a sad point we heard to different extents in the five countries where we interviewed individuals. Namely, countries and relief agencies tend to settle families with refugee experiences in some of their poorest and most violent neighbourhoods, places where trauma continues to be created. While this reality emerged most strongly in our American interviews, it was also a thread that appeared in Northern Ireland, Australia, and England.

Just as early childhood educators need to be aware of the trauma experienced by families prior to arriving in the host country, it is also necessary to understand the communities in which these families settle. Young children who are exposed to poverty, violence, and deprivation are affected negatively. Often educators do not live in the communities they serve, and they would be well informed by taking the time to explore the neighbourhoods in which their students live. Being cognisant of the challenges families face helps educators identify potential causes of changes in behaviour and performance. Toxic stress, as Montgomery (2010) cautions, can have debilitating effects. A further point about resettlement is that large populations of newly arrived families are often placed in the same apartments and communities. While this concentration of individuals with refugee backgrounds can offer families support, it can also come with a host of challenges. Large numbers of people who are attempting to integrate, learn a new language, find work, navigate new cultures and schooling, and process their own traumatic histories likely create a stressful environment and produce additional anxiety for sensitive young children. For those who serve young children, understanding these complexities is key to building care.

Breaking the cycle

While it does appear that changes to the ways in which genes behave (epigenetics) and the ways in which DNA is interpreted are reversible with corresponding changes in environment, stress levels, lifestyle, and well-being (Fitzgerald et al., 2021), there has been a dedicated attempt to break the cycle for adolescent mothers by educating them to be aware of the symptoms and transmission processes of intergenerational trauma (Chokshi et al., 2023). In this study, Generational Trauma Cards (GTC) were developed using comic-type images and small speech bubbles, along with other visual effects to simply explain the ways in which trauma is passed from one generation to another and the negative impacts of this process. The participants demonstrated that they understood the purpose and meaning of the GTCs and they planned on positively sharing the information to others and to monitoring their own responses to parenthood and its stresses. They indicated that they would prioritise their own self-care in addition to their baby's, be aware of their emotional lives and mental health, utilising mindfulness strategies, accessing healthcare workers and support groups, and taking time to process trauma itself. A review of the literature that focuses on intergenerational trauma (Isobel et al., 2019), found that interventions of various types were the key to preventing transmission of trauma from one generation to another. While they emphasised two major constructs that needed to be addressed – (i) resolving parental trauma and (ii) actively supporting parent–infant attachment – they concluded:

> Prevention is the most effective intervention approach for intergenerational transmission of trauma. Prevention requires trauma-specific interventions with adults and attachment-focused interventions within families. Preventative strategies need to target individual, relationship, familial, community and societal levels, as addressing and preventing trauma requires a multi-pronged, multisystemic approach.
>
> (Isobel et al., 2019, p. 1100)

While this may, at first glance, appear to be outside the realm of those who educate and care for the young and the very young, it is an integral part of their professional work. There are multiple opportunities for childcare workers and teachers to support parents and their wider communities and to facilitate improved mother–child attachments. One of these may be negotiating cultural differences in childcare, nurture, and expectations at various development stages, another may be challenging racist, discriminatory, and 'othering' practices at systemic, institutional, and individual levels of their workplaces (Arar et al., 2019; Brooks & Watson, 2019; Foucault, 1979; Foucault, 1991; Said, 1978).

Research findings

A shared imperative among many of our research participants was a strong desire to advocate on behalf of the people they serve. We spoke with a primary principal in England and a migrant support worker in Australia who shared anecdotes about supporting newly arrived families and breaking the cycle of trauma.

> *Context:* I'm the principal of a primary school. It's in a deprived part of [England]. We've also got a really strong moral and political imperative for the work that we do, which is about smashing the glass ceilings that I know society puts into place for communities like ours. You know, they talk

a really good talk about wanting to create opportunities. Actually, a lot of people don't really want brown, black Muslim poor white people living next to them. But we do.

We have a strong view that there's no place in our community, our school and our world for racism, for prejudice, or judgment. But a couple of, probably 2 or 3 years ago, one of the children had a bike. Their bike disappeared from outside the school, and one of the teachers said one of the Romanian families stole a lot. Oh, fuck it! I'm sorry, I swear a lot. So, I challenged him, and we made it a whole school thing. Is that okay to say that? To label all of our Romanian families as thieves? Of course, it's not!

Context: I have been working with migrant families for a very long time in Australia. I spent years working in and managing childcare centres and now I work with centres to help them better support children. I earned my master's degree years ago in early childhood education. I tell staff it is important that we not try to fix families, that we learn all we can about families.

Life is very hard, and therefore children sometimes might exhibit that behaviour. They'll play with guns and show violence; that's a sign of strong fighting for my place in this world. That takes time for educators to understand that you know it's not the gun. It's what you will be doing and how we help families understand or observe that child's behaviour rather than immediately jumping to say, 'Oh, look! You know he's playing with another child by pretending with the stickies again, because police use guns, right?' And you know, that was so we just need to be mindful of how we interpret that behaviour.

Unique contexts, global principles

Though half a world apart, our two educators share a belief that part of their job is to work with local communities to help remove barriers for newly arrived families and ease the ongoing trauma families may be experiencing in their new settings. Our English primary principal was blunt in her assessment that many people do not want refugees, particularly racial minorities, living in their communities, and actively place roadblocks in front of them. Her vignette about the teacher who assigned blame for a stolen bike to the school's Romanian population is both appalling and informative. While she rightly took a robust stance against an individual promoting racist stereotypes, the vignette also shows racism can emanate from an employee within a school or any organisation. Our Australian support worker pushed her educators to be thoughtful in examining and understanding children's behaviour. In the vignette she shared, rather than assuming children with refugee backgrounds might be using stick guns to imitate police officers, she challenged her preschool staff members to understand the child in question may be responding to lived violence or attempting to assert himself by pretending to take some modicum of control on the playground. In both cases, our participants offer a call for educators to look beyond superficial or stereotypical ideas to truly support families.

By its very definition, intergenerational trauma is long-lasting and destructive for many individuals. Our research pointed to the importance of good people taking strong stands to help diminish the longevity of intergenerational trauma. Undoubtedly, racism, stereotyping, and bigotry exist in all countries and can make the resettlement journey of newly arrived families much more challenging. Carers who are willing to call out these cancerous practices contribute to the easing of intergenerational trauma. Our first research vignette was telling in that our participant had to defend her newly arrived families against external and internal detractors. While an unsupportive community is destructive, few things can be as corrosive for an organisation as employees who do not support the mission or who work to undermine the stakeholders served. Preschool directors, principals, and individuals who run any organisation supporting families with refugee backgrounds need to often remind staff of the mission, ensure they are supportive, and counsel individuals out if they do not share in the mission. Coupled with this advocacy, leaders must remind their staff members of the often superficial and inaccurate nature of stereotyping behaviours. Just as our second research participant suggested playing with sticks was perhaps more than boys emulating police officers, educators should be encouraged to stop and ask 'why?' children or families are behaving in a particular way. As with so many aspects of supporting families with refugee backgrounds, being curious, seeking additional information, and reflecting are vital to helping moderate the effects of intergenerational trauma.

Conclusion

Understanding the causes, consequences, and ways to address intergenerational trauma is important for those who support families with refugee experiences. Young children living with parents processing grief feel their parents' despair acutely and are likely to present negative emotional, behavioural, or academic concerns. Our participants shared vignettes of families living with fear and anxiety from years spent in refugee camps and they told of families being resettled in dangerous neighbourhoods in their host countries. For carers, understanding the home lives of the young children they work with can help to pinpoint causes of behaviour and offer possible avenues for support. Beyond educating young children, our research also points to the need for early childhood staff to be advocates for the families they serve. Calling out racism, creating organisations that are fully committed to the families they serve, and looking beyond superficial understandings of human beings and human behaviour are work that will reduce the cycle of intergenerational trauma.

References

Ager, A., & Strang, A. (2008). Understanding integration: A conceptual framework. *Journal of Refugee Studies, 21*(2), 166–191. https://doi.org/10.1093/jrs/fen016

Alemi, Q., & Stempel, C. (2018). Discrimination and distress among Afghan refugees in northern California: The moderating role of pre- and post-migration factors. *PLoS One, 13*(5), e0196822. https://doi.org/10.1371/journal.pone.0196822

Alhassen, S., Chen, S., Alhassen, L., Phan, A., Khoudari, M., De Silva, A., Barhoosh, H., Wang, Z., Parrocha, C., Shapiro, E., Henrich, C., Wang, Z., Mutesa, L., Baldi, P., Abbott, G. W., & Alachkar, A. (2021). Intergenerational trauma transmission is associated with brain metabotranscriptome remodeling and mitochondrial dysfunction. *Communications Biology, 4*(1). https://doi.org/10.1038/s42003-021-02255-2

Arar, K., Brooks, J., & Bogotch, I. (2019). *Education, immigration and migration policy, leadership and praxis for a changing world.* Emerald Publishing.

Baak, M. (2019). Racism and othering for South Sudanese heritage students in Australian schools: Is inclusion possible? *International Journal of Inclusive Education, 23*(2), 125–141. https://doi.org/10.1080/13603116.2018.1426052

Beiser, M., & Hou, F. (2016). Mental health effects of premigration trauma and post-migration discrimination on refugee youth in Canada. *The Journal of Nervous and Mental Disease, 204*(6), 464–470. DOI: 10.1097/NMD.0000000000000516

Berry, J. (1997). Immigration, acculturation, and adaptation. *Applied Psychology: An International Review, 46*(1), 5–68.

Berry, J. (2001). A psychology of immigration. *Journal of Social Issues, 7*(3), 615–631.

Berry, J., Phinney, J., Sam, D., & Vedder, P. (2006). Immigrant youth: Acculturation, identity, and adaptation. *Applied Psychology: An International Review, 55*(3), 303–332.

Bombay, A., Matheson, K., & Anisman, H. (2009). Intergenerational trauma: Convergence of multiple processes among first nations peoples in Canada. *International Journal of Indigenous Health, 5*(3), 6–47.

Bornstein, M. H. (2012). Cultural approaches to parenting. *Parenting, 12*(2–3), 212–221. https://doi.org/10.1080/15295192.2012.683359

Bowers, M. E., & Yehuda, R. (2016). Intergenerational transmission of stress in humans. *Neuropsychopharmacology, 41*(1), 232–244. https://doi.org/10.1038/npp.2015.247

Brooks, J., & Watson, T. (2019). School leadership and racism: An ecological perspective. *Urban Education, 54*(5), 631–655. https://doi.org/10.1177/0042085918783821

Buonagurio, N. (2020). The cycle continues: The effects of intergenerational trauma on the sense of self and the healing opportunities of dance movement therapy: A literature review. https://digitalcommons.lesley.edu/cgi/viewcontent.cgi?article=1283&context=expressive_theses

Carlile, A. (2012). An ethnography of permanent exclusion from school: Revealing and untangling the threads of institutionalised racism. *Race Ethnicity and Education, 15*(2), 175–194. https://doi.org/10.1080/13613324.2010.548377

Chokshi, B., Pukatch, C., Ramsey, N., Dzienny, A., & Smiley, Y. (2023). The generational trauma card: A tool to educate on intergenerational trauma transmission. *Journal of Loss and Trauma, 28*(5), 464–471. https://doi.org/10.1080/15325024.2022.2091315

Davidson, N., Skull, S., Burgner, D., Kelly, P., Raman, S., Silove, D., Steel, Z., Vora, R., & Smith, M. (2004). An issue of access: Delivering equitable health care for newly arrived refugee children in Australia. *Journal of Paediatrics and Child Health*, *40*(9–10), 569–575.

Deng, S. A., & Marlowe, J. M. (2013). Refugee resettlement and parenting in a different context. *Journal of Immigrant & Refugee Studies*, *11*(4), 416–430. https://doi.org/10.1080/15562948.2013.793441

Dozio, E., Feldman, M., Bizouerne, C., Drain, E., Laroche Joubert, M., Mansouri, M., Moro, M. R., & Ouss, L. (2020). The transgenerational transmission of trauma: The effects of maternal PTSD in mother–infant interactions. *Frontiers in Psychiatry*, *11*, 480690. https://doi.org/10.3389/fpsyt.2020.480690

Ellis, B. H., MacDonald, H. Z., Lincoln, A. K., & Cabral, H. J. (2008). Mental health of Somali adolescent refugees: The role of trauma, stress, and perceived discrimination. *Journal of Consulting and Clinical Psychology*, *76*(2). https://doi.org/10.1037/0022-006X.76.2.184

Fitzgerald, K. N., Hodges, R., Hanes, D., Stack, E., Cheishvili, D., Szyf, M., Henkel, J., Twedt, M. W., Giannopoulou, D., Herdell, J., Logan, S., & Bradley, R. (2021). Potential reversal of epigenetic age using a diet and lifestyle intervention: A pilot randomized clinical trial. *Aging*, *13*(7), 9419–9432. https://doi.org/10.18632/aging.202913

Foucault, M. (1979). *Power, truth, strategy*. Feral Publications.

Foucault, M. (1991). Governmentality. In B. Burchell, G. Gordon, & B. Miller (Eds.), *The Foucault effect: Studies in governmentality*. Chicago University Press.

Goodnow, J. J. (2014). Refugees, asylum seekers, displaced persons: Children in precarious positions. In G. B. Melton, A. Ben-Arieh, J. Cashmore, G. S. Goodman, & N. K. Worley (Eds.), *The SAGE handbook of child research* (pp. 339–360). SAGE Publications.

Gopalkrishnan, N. (2018). Cultural diversity and mental health: Considerations for policy and practice. *Frontiers in Public Health*, *6*, 179. https://doi.org/10.3389/fpubh.2018.00179

Gronski, M. P., Bogan, K. E., Kloeckner, J., Russell-Thomas, D., Taff, S. D., Walker, K. A., & Berg, C. (2013). Childhood toxic stress: A community role in health promotion for occupational therapists. *American Journal of Occupational Therapy*, *67*(6), e148–e153.

Hechanova, M. R. M., Waelde, L. C., & Torres, A. N. (2020). Cultural implications for the provision of disaster mental health and psychosocial support in Southeast Asia. In M. R. M. Hechanova & L. C. Waelde (Eds.), *Resistance, resilience, and recovery from disasters: Perspectives from Southeast Asia* (Vol. 21, pp. 3–13). Emerald Publishing Limited. https://doi.org/10.1108/S2040-726220200000021001

Henley, J., & Robinson, J. (2011). Mental health issues among refugee children and adolescents. *Clinical Psychologist*, *15*(2), 51–62. https://doi.org/10.1111/j.1742-9552.2011.00024.x

Hernandez, M., Nesman, T., Mowery, D., Acevedo-Polakovich, I. D., & Callejas, L. M. (2009). Cultural competence: A literature review and conceptual model for mental health services. *Psychiatric Services*, *60*(8), 1046–1050. https://doi.org/10.1176/ps.2009.60.8.1046

Hofstede, G. (2001). *Culture's consequences: Comparing values, behaviors, institutions and organizations across nations* (2nd ed.). Sage.

Hofstede, G. (2011). Dimensionalizing cultures: The Hofstede model in context. *Online Readings in Psychology and Culture, 2,* 1–26.

Hofstede, G., Hofstede, G. J., & Minkov, M. (2010). *Cultures and organisations: Software of the mind.* McGraw-Hill.

Isobel, S., Goodyear, M., Furness, T., & Foster, K. (2019). Preventing intergenerational trauma transmission: A critical interpretive synthesis. *Journal of Clinical Nursing, 28*(7–8), 1100–1113. https://doi.org/10.1111/jocn.14735

Lewig, K., Arney, F., & Salveron, M. (2010). Challenges to parenting in a new culture: Implications for child and family welfare. *Evaluation and Program Planning, 33*(3), 324–332. https://doi.org/10.1016/j.evalprogplan.2009.05.002

Lustig, S. L., Kia-Keating, M., Knight, W. G., Geltman, P., Ellis, H., Kinzie, J. D., Keane, T., & Saxe, G. N. (2004). Review of child and adolescent refugee mental health. *Journal of the American Academy of Child & Adolescent Psychiatry, 43*(1), 24–36. https://doi.org/10.1097/00004583-200401000-00012

Masten, A. S. (2014). Global perspectives on resilience in children and youth. *Child Development, 85*(1), 6–20.

Masten, A. S. (2016). Resilience in developing systems: The promise of integrated approaches. *European Journal of Developmental Psychology, 13*(3), 297–312. https://doi.org/10.1080/17405629.2016.1147344

Masten, A. S., & Shaffer, A. (2006). How families matter in child development: Reflections from research on risk and resilience. In A. Clarke-Stewart & J. Dunn (Eds.), *Families count: Effects on child and adolescent development* (pp. 5–25). Cambridge University Press.

McCarty, T. L., & Wyman, L. T. (2009). Indigenous youth and bilingualism: Theory, research, praxis. *Journal of Language, Identity, and Education, 8*(5), 279–290.

Menzies, P. (2010). Intergenerational trauma from a mental health perspective. *Native Social Work Journal, 7,* 63–85.

Migliarini, V. (2017). 'Colour-evasiveness' and racism without race: The disablement of asylum-seeking children at the edge of fortress Europe. *Race Ethnicity and Education, 21*(4), 438–457. https://doi.org/10.1080/13613324.2017.1417252

Montgomery, E. (2010). Trauma and resilience in young refugees: A 9-year follow-up study. *Development and Psychopathology, 22*(2), 477–489. https://doi.org/10.1017/S0954579410000180

Montgomery, E. (2011). Trauma, exile and mental health in young refugees. *Acta Psychiatrica Scandinavica, 124,* 1–46. https://doi.org/10.1111/j.1600-0447.2011.01740.x

Napolitano, F., Gualdieri, L., Santagati, G., & Angelillo, I. F. (2018). Violence experience among immigrants and refugees: A cross-sectional study in Italy. *BioMed Research International, 2018,* 7949483. https://doi.org/10.1155/2018/7949483

O'Brien, M., & Hoffstaedter, G. (2020). "There we are nothing, here we are nothing!": The enduring effects of the Rohingya genocide. *Social Sciences, 9*(11), 209. https://doi.org/10.3390/socsci9110209

Raphael, B., Swan, P., & Martinek, N. (1998). Intergenerational aspects of trauma for Australian aboriginal people. In Y. Danieli (Ed.), *International handbook of multigenerational legacies of trauma* (pp. 327–339). Springer.

Said, E. (1978). Introduction. *Orientalism*. Vintage Books.

Schechter, D. (2010). Multigenerational ataques de nervios in a Dominician-American family: A form of intergenerational transmission of violent trauma. In C. Worthman, P. Plotsky, D. Schechter, & C. Cummings (Eds.), *Formative experiences: The interaction of caregiving, culture and developmental psychobiology*. Cambridge University Press.

Stargel, L., & Easterbrooks, A. (2020). Diversity of adverse childhood experiences among adolescent mothers and the intergenerational transmission of risk to children's behavior problems. *Social Science & Medicine*, *250*, 112828. https://doi.org/10.1016/j.socscimed.2020.112828

Sun, J., Patel, F., Rose-Jacobs, R., Frank, D. A., Black, M. M., & Chilton, M. (2017). Mothers' adverse childhood experiences and their young children's development. *American Journal of Preventive Medicine*, *53*(6), 882–891. https://doi.org/10.1016/j.amepre.2017.07.015

Tribe, R. (2002). Mental health of refugees and asylum-seekers. *ROAR*, *8*(4), 240–248.

Uvin, P. (2003). Reading the Rwandan genocide. *International Studies Review*, *3*(3), 75–99. https://doi.org/10.1111/1521-9488.00245

Van Ee, E., Kleber, R. J., & Mooren, T. T. (2012). War trauma lingers on: Associations between maternal posttraumatic stress disorder, parent–child interaction, and child development. *Infant Mental Health Journal*, *33*(5), 459–468. https://doi.org/10.1002/imhj.21324

White, J., de Quadros, A., & Kelman, D. (2017). Belonging and rejection: Racism, resistance and exclusion. *International Journal of Inclusive Education*, *21*(11), 1081–1082. https://doi.org/10.1080/13603116.2017.1350315

Yehuda, R., & Lehrner, A. (2018). Intergenerational transmission of trauma effects: Putative role of epigenetic mechanisms. *World Psychiatry*, *17*(3), 243–257. https://doi.org/10.1002/wps.20568

Chapter 8

Successful early childhood transitions and school readiness

Introduction

Early childhood educators working with migrant and refugee children face many challenges. They must create learning environments that support the developmental needs of the children in their care, many of whom have experienced trauma; work to build trust with recently resettled families; develop sensitivities to the host cultures of those families; and even support families as they transition to their new homes, communities, and cultures. As if this set of responsibilities was not daunting enough, early educators are also guiding the children in their care along the pathway to school readiness and later academic success. This chapter will consider the concept of school readiness, and the special challenges the transition to formal schooling present for early childhood educators working with migrant and refugee children.

Transitioning to school

Successful transitions to school are highly dependent on what is generally known as 'school readiness.' This term almost exclusively applied to the competencies and capacities that young children *should* have developed by the time they are enrolled in mandatory schooling (High & AAP, 2008; Lewit & Baker, 1995; Pan et al., 2019; Potmesilova & Potmesil, 2021). With the exception of those children identified with documented medical disorders and learning difficulties, these attributes are predominately regarded as social and emotional skills and maturity, physical and health markers, and language and cognitive proficiencies. However, school readiness can be considered more literally in the context of how schools are ready to welcome, accommodate, and meet the needs of diverse learners with heterogeneous experiences, dissimilar backgrounds, and a wide variety of expectations (Williams et al., 2019). The current climate of political and economic neoliberalism that is dominant in some form throughout English-speaking countries such as those from which the participants were drawn has filtered through into education systems, their status as funded institutions, and their purpose in society. They prioritise productivity, economies, and efficiencies. They not only reflect factory models, but they also incorporate the standardisation of benchmarking, the explicit grading of products and the preservation of social status (Bourdieu, 1986, 1990), and the narrowing of curriculum and pedagogies as reflections of neoliberal ideals. These systemic, institutional, educational institutions are defined by five major characteristics, each of which impact on the potential of the school to be prepared to authentically integrate newcomer students into their communities. Although they appear disparate, these characteristics work together to support each other in weaving the face and fabric of neoliberal schooling. These characteristics can be described as the five C's; Competitiveness, Conformity, Conservatism, Convention, and Commerce (Sellars & Imig, 2020a), each of which can present hurdles and barriers to the full inclusion of students who are not of the majority culture and which may raise concerns for students of refugee and asylum-seeker backgrounds and their parents.

Competitiveness is a characteristic of individualistic societies (Geert Hofstede, 2011; Hofstede et al., 2010; Minkov et al., 2017). In these contexts, individuals are expected to be self-reliant, to have personal opinions, and to have less reliance on the cohesion of groups. They strive for success and achievement as personal accomplishments. These educational contexts favour standardised testing, promoting the grading of students against each other and against benchmarks, assuming therefore that all students grow cognitively at the same rate, have the same experiences and opportunities, and the same resources, both human and material to support them. Integral to success in these contexts are the capabilities to culturally and socially navigate the language, structure, and context of what is required and respond appropriately, necessitating the need for all students to bow to the *conformity* of a specific mode of communication, irrespective of the differences of context, time, and space (Hall, 1976) as responses to the narrowly defined epistemology that is considered valuable and measurable by those with the power to determine the educational agenda (Ball, 2016; Biesta & Miedema, 2002; Shahjahan, 2011). *Conservatism*, most particularly Eurocentric conservatism, dominates the pedagogical practices of this paradigm, focusing on economy and efficiency and reflecting the experiences of those dominating in this factory model, using predefined outcomes as measures of success and accountability, leading to the inevitability of the 10% product failure rate maintained to legitimise all sound industrial models. This is, in turn, demanded by the operational *conventions* of the systems. While these are most frequently based on unstable foundations and traditions, they are nevertheless significant factors of school life and reflect the routines and regulations of historical practice, irrespective of cultural and social diversity and norms, interfamilial practices, and individual student needs. These characteristics or dimensions of neoliberalised education systems combine to promote the overarching purpose of this educational paradigm, which is to train and develop individuals exclusively for the workplace, that is, to serve the purposes of those invested in *commerce*. Critical to the philosophy of free trade and survival of the fittest, neoliberal schooling interpolates these five characteristics to train young people to become the 'human capital' upon which economy-focused societies depend.

Research findings

Across the world, schools, preschools, and even day care centres are operated under the shadow of neoliberal practices and policies. These practices can challenge the efforts of well-meaning people attempting to support the transition of newly arrived students into new settings. We spoke with a preschool coordinator in Australia and a preschool director in Northern Ireland who provided valuable insights about the process.

Context: I am a pre-school coordinator. Our center is located in the heart of the [refugee] community. We can recruit educators who speak those languages. They can do that, and it works. I think it is better for them because you have staff members from that community. We have South Sudanese, moving from Melbourne and North Sudanese and a lot of Mongolians. After what happened in Afghanistan last year, America's pulling out was very predictable, we knew there would be a huge influx into Australia as part of the resettlement program. They were spread out and a whole group came to [our city].

Any child who goes to preschool they do have teachers and so on. My daughter had to put her own winter jacket on. She had to look after her own backpack, things, and belongings. That's how they're going to compete with society and other children. They need to have this basic instinct, so they don't get bullied, don't fall behind, and they're confident. They're able to talk to the teachers with that sense of confidence, it doesn't have to be perfect English, but they should be able to have that confidence. Raise your hand and say, 'Excuse me.' We tell the children all the time if someone is doing something, if you don't like it, stop it. That's what we teach. Kids in daycare are in school, so use your voice. Sometimes, it's their first English. The speech is 'Stop it. I don't like it.' That's what we're doing, this part of the resettlement program. Our job is to make these kids settled in Australia and within the Australian culture. I'm doing the same thing I did with my own girls.

Context: I'm relatively new to the preschool program but on my feet quite well. We have two classes of about 25 children. So the school has a wide range of nationalities, abilities, and needs. I think as the years go on, more special needs are coming through, particularly the newcomers. For children who have special needs, it's sometimes a bit harder to identify because of the language barrier.

To integrate families, we try to get our families into school as much as we can from the start of the year. We've had play and stay days with the parents, and we're having sessions with the parents with planting and gardening, so it's open to everybody to come in. We also have a program starting for parents. A lot of the newcomers have said they're going to come. It's led by myself and another staff member, and it goes through like reading with your child, counting with your child, that kind of thing. So just bringing them in with no barriers is a big thing, making them feel welcome and integrated into the school. It is such a big thing. Having everything open to them, the doors open so they can come in and speak to us. We have to be approachable and make them feel comfortable to come in and talk to them about anything. We have to have a good relationship with them. You know that's the key.

Unique contexts, global principles

These early educators shared vital observations about some of the skills young children should have ready in order to make successful transition to kindergarten and formal schooling. In the first instance, our respondent is a leader in a stand-alone preschool programme, who also is able to share her perspective as a mother, and a migrant to Australia. This teacher reflects on the knowledge young children need to have at almost an instinctual level in order to most successfully transition to kindergarten. These skills include a level of self-confidence, and a set of interpersonal skills that will allow her to advocate for herself, both in claiming space and respect from her classmates and in asking for help and otherwise interacting with her teachers. Our research participant from Northern Ireland is a preschool teacher working within a public school setting. She cautions to remember that many children who are newcomers may have special needs, and those needs often will be extremely difficult to identify where there are also language barriers to navigate. She also highlights the importance of easing the transition for both young children and their parents and families. Towards that end, she outlines a number of strategies for making those parents and children feel welcome.

In both of these cases, our respondents hint at the difficult path newly arrived families and young children must navigate when they first arrive in an unfamiliar country. Try as we might to develop sensitivities to cultural differences, children will find themselves in new situations where their ingrained understandings and conditioned responses may fail them. Learning to speak up for themselves with classmates, and learning how to ask for help from teachers, for example, are important skills that will increasingly come into play as they transition from preschool to more formal school settings. Parents, as a child's first and most important teachers, can be enlisted as allies in making this transition to school a success. As our second participant suggests, recruiting parents is key to this vital effort. Educators may consider offering play-and-stay times for families, scheduling special programmes for parents and families beyond traditional school hours, and making it profoundly clear parents are welcome to visit during the school day.

What are the implications?

Unfortunately, education systems appear to be dominated by notions that not only contradict but seek to pervert what educational research across many knowledge domains has been finding for decades (Ball, 2016; Biesta, 2014; Biesta & Miedema, 2002; Gary, 2016). The current cycles of standardised testing that is testament to highly competitive nature of schooling disadvantages students in several ways from the outset. It implies that all children learn at the same rate, in linear fashion, according to chronological age. For students with refugee and asylum-seeker backgrounds, there are multiple problems with this aspect of school. Developmental delays in cognition that may be the result of complex childhood trauma, intergenerational trauma, poverty-related circumstances, paucity of rich learning experiences, limited English language skills are among the many complexities that may hinder the progress of these children when entering the competitive school system. Conformity presents itself in many guises in school environments. Most critically, to support the competitive nature of schools, it demands that only certain types of knowledge, skills, and expertise are valued and celebrated. The emphasis is not on what children can do, how they may have diverse ways of knowing and doing, but that they focus on how well they can learn, in prescribed ways, the preselected, narrow curricula that is privileged as knowledge. This is particularly disadvantageous for children with backgrounds of oracy (Coultas, 2015; Rosa & Orey, 2015). Neoliberal schooling also must be efficient and economical. In many cases this results in young children being subjected to an exclusive diet of 'one size fits all,' direct instruction under many guises, with little differentiation in the way of alternative pathways, working with student strengths and interests or valuing the intellectual capital they bring to the classroom (Sellars, 2008, 2014, 2020). Much of what is culturally valued in the diverse home environments is neglected, or at worst, challenged as being insignificant, without value, or nonsensical.

The entire notion of how schools operate, the expectations that are implicit in the notion of agreed-upon, culturally narrow, society-specific conventions, pervade every aspect of institutional life and pose a considerable barrier to those who do not recognise them, understand them, or who disagree with them. Implicit or tacit knowledge, whether conceptual or procedural, is generally accepted to be knowledge that is unconsciously learned. Students with this tacit knowledge have been found to be more successful at school (Zheyu et al., 2021). Embedded in individual school routines and requirements are numerous regulations relating to context, time, and space, many of which may be unfamiliar to students from other cultures. These may relate to who does what, where, when, and how. Everyday matters such as use of facilities such as toilets, expectations of table manners and traditions around when and how food is eaten at school, what is provided for school dinners, what and how school uniform (or other clothing) may be worn or altered are mandated. Means of communicating are also subjected to school culture in addition to the diversity of codes and taboos dictated by religious and cultural belief systems (Hall, 1976). Convention is also apparent in systemic and legislative matters relating to schooling. Most significantly for these students, the use of chronological age to determine when they must start school and into which class they must be placed, irrespective of their developmental status, emotional maturity, or their capacities to regulate themselves and conform to other school requirements. These may include sitting for prescribed periods on chairs, at desks, listening without moving or speaking for lengthy intervals. These dimensions work together to establish the purpose of neoliberal education which is to prepare the young for the workforce where many will serve the interests of the few at the top in the world of commerce.

Research findings

Like all people, families with refugee experiences have experiences, beliefs, likes, and practices that have shaped their lives. When these families arrive in new countries, their cultural backgrounds are often marginalised to make room for the host culture. We gained understandings from an American educator who currently directs her state's early childhood professional development programmes and an American resettlement agency employee in a mid-size city that has seen a large influx of families with refugee backgrounds.

> *Context:* I've taught graduate courses in early childhood education, run a childcare center and even owned a center. I can't retire. Currently, I am the program manager for our state's early childhood professional development and learning hub.

> Another example, we had a family, an Asian family. We had a lot of Asian families. They said their toddler, probably around a year old, likes noodles every day. And, the teachers made food for the children. But, the parents brought noodles and wanted this baby to eat noodles. The teachers kept giving this baby American food like macaroni and cheese, and chicken nuggets, which the baby loved. But, the parents were very upset; this was not what they wanted. They wanted noodles fed to this child. It wasn't done out of ignorance or being harmful, like the teachers don't want to do what the parents want them to do. But there's a real dynamic in early childhood where the teachers feel like they know better. It's almost that ugly American thing, I may only be 19 or 20 years old, but I'm American, and I know better for this baby.

Context: I work for a resettlement agency and one of our requirements is to only enroll children in schools with ESL support within that school. And so sometimes that means we are enrolling kids in schools that they are not zoned for or different things like that, but we have to make sure that there are specific supports around language accommodation and other things like that, and then we try to supplement through orientation and training through that. But transportation is not provided, so that's an additional barrier.

I think one of the most bizarre calls I have received during school was I had a set of brothers that didn't know how to use toilet paper, and their mum sent them with a special water bottle that was matched for toilet use, and it completely unnerved the teacher. She had no idea how to handle that cultural hygiene practice and what that meant and was just really disturbed. And so trying to navigate that with the teacher and a parent and trying to like come up with a happy compromise. And so I think we landed on the kids going to the school with wet wipes, which was an appropriate compromise that the school and the family could make.

Unique contexts, global principles

The first vignette presented above is particularly telling as it shares the friction between a teacher and family over toddler feeding practices. In the second, friction surfaced around cultural differences and expectations in terms of toileting norms. These vignettes highlight some of the ways cultural norms and differences can run afoul of institutionally mandated uniformity and public school norms in many Western societies. In both of these stories, family perceptions of what is best for their own young children were different from school norms. Those expectations emerged from each family's cultural backgrounds. Acceptable in contexts where they were the norm, these different cultural practices became problematic when they represented a deviation from standard practices in settings that serve large numbers of children, leading to tensions between centre staff and parents.

While it is debatable whether a steady diet of noodles or of chicken nuggets is preferable, the broader point concerns the degree to which an institution is obligated, or inclined, to respect cultural norms that challenge its functioning and usual ways of operating. Should centre staff be obligated to warm and serve a special meal for a specific child, or does it better serve the mission of the centre for newly arrived students to eat the same foods prepared and served to every other child in the school? Likewise, the issue of toileting practices highlights the ways cultural differences can be extremely challenging to Western visions of uniformity in schooling. Within Western systems built on conformity, which are often concerned with providing a perception of equal treatment to all students, many school leaders have little patience or latitude when it comes to brokering solutions to cultural differences like these that will be acceptable to all parties. This is where the opportunity for further education, creative thinking, and a willingness to push up against policy arises. Directors and principals may find it helpful to educate their, often young, staff members about the families they serve and collectively brainstorm strategies that both respect and support the integration of these families.

Bringing school and student together

A key aspect of successful school transition for children and parents with refugee and asylum-seeker backgrounds is the relationship that is formed from the very first meeting. How the enrolment process is conducted and by whom is a key element in setting the scene for all future interactions and the development of relationships. One participant shared his practice. Despite having to commit to a hectic schedule of duties as a school principal, he understood the importance placed on teachers, and especially school leaders by many members of the refugee community. Working with the SCARF (Rock, 2008; Rock & Cox, 2012) principles in mind, he undertook the enrolment of these students himself. This frequently included working with interpreters and other community members sensitively, conducting a tour of the school, and ensuring the free uniform and other school equipment met the cultural and religious expectations of the parents or caregivers. This was a particularly important and sensitive issue for girls' uniforms. The SCARF model was developed in the context of business management but is equally applicable to the relationships that can be identified as positive school culture and ethos (Alder, 1993; Donnelly, 2000; Glover & Coleman, 2005; McLaughlin, 2005; Sellars, 2021; Solvason, 2005). By implementing the SCARF model as a school philosophy, this principal was able to take consistent steps to ensure that decisions made by himself, and all the staff reflected the affirmative actions embedded in the acronym. *Status* is a critical aspect of belonging and acceptance. The strategies that were put in place to establish Status for these resettlement families included the provision of a parent cafe (Bradley & Sellars, 2021), a conscious decision to adapt to the traditional means of communication and decision-making in diverse cultures, and sensitivity to aspects of communication such as body language, personal space, and facial expression among many other everyday of respect. This status was acknowledged from the first contact with them. In the lengthy enrolment interviews he held, he advised the parents to ensure that their children spoke their first language at least four days every week at home and spoke only English at home on the other three days. He felt it was important for the students to respect and acknowledge their homeland cultures. The consistency with which these parents and their children were received and valued as members of the school community lead to the feeling of trust and *Certainty*.

Certainty is a rewarding and pleasurable experience. In cases of uncertainty, the brain must work harder to make meaning of the unexpected, causing distraction from the goal in action until it is resolved. Having clear expectations of community members in all aspects of the educational environment allowed the school staff and families with refugee and asylum-seeker experiences to be reliably welcoming and consolidate the development of trust and belonging. These strategies did not go unnoticed by the school community who welcomed and celebrated them. This led to the increasing sense of *Autonomy* that was created for these parents who, to date, had little, if any, choice available to them since their displacement. In educational environments, 'voice and choice' are recognised as being powerful motivators for engagements and productivity (Bragg, 2016; Mitchell et al., 2015). While giving members of the community opportunities to make decisions about becoming involved in school activities, joining teams or working alone may appear to limit autonomy, it is in making the choice available that perceptions of autonomy can be realised. Team-building and collaborative actions also provide experiences which raise levels of *Relatedness,* as these forms of 'coming together' cooperatively allow individuals to belong to social circles and working groups. *Relatedness* is experienced as friendships, acceptance, and interactions with people who are trustworthy in the estimation of the individual involved. It can also be described as in (or conversely out of) a social or professional group of people. The notion of belonging or inclusion is identified as a basic human need, proposed to be as basic as food and shelter (Cacioppo & Patrick, 2008). The final component of the acronym is *Fairness.* This Fairness can be demonstrated by having clear guidelines and expectations, and, in classroom contexts, by the students developing the rules and guidelines for expectations and behaviours themselves. The SCARF model, with sensitive and informed implementation, may support the development of school ethos and culture that explicitly promotes inclusivity and belonging which are among the trademarks of pedagogical love. Pedagogical love has been an educational construct for over two centuries (Sellars & Imig, 2020b). It is described by Gidley (2016, pp. 181–186) as 'evolutionary,' by Chabot (2008) as transformative power, and by Kaukko et al. (2021) as genuinely caring acts to which principals must aspire and achieve to meet the needs of students with refugee experiences. Pedagogical love is the antithesis of all that neoliberal influences in education (the Five C characteristics) represent.

Many of the students with refugee and asylum-seeker experiences originate from collectivist cultures (Hofstede, 1986, 2001; Hofstede, 2011). While attitudes on child-rearing, play, and other cultural characteristics may differ among the generalised term of 'collectivist cultures' resulting in some children being extremely reliant on adult assistance with basic tasks while being capable of sitting still and listening for extended periods of time, for example, while children from other collectivist cultures are more self-reliant but unable to concentrate for long. While there may be many reasons other than cultural for a variety of diverse behaviours and cognitive capacities, including the impacts of complex childhood trauma, intergenerational trauma, and familial and individual characteristics, some general dimensions may be apparent. Members of collectivist cultures, by their nature, are heavily invested in belonging. They are group- and family-orientated, which makes the efforts of school principals and staff increasingly significant in school interactions. They also share the dimension of power distance. This means that people are accustomed to a hierarchical order in society which does not require any justification, everyone has their place on the ladder. This results in the automatic acceptance of the principal and others as people of authority to be impressed and not to be questioned or disrespected. This may even extend to students in class not asking questions from the teacher as it may imply that they had not been teaching successfully. Their loyalty extends to taking responsibility for all members of the group as 'losing face' and 'shaming' are felt by all members of the group if transgressions occur. Many collectivist countries are masculine in nature, which means not only some male dominance, but also that strong decision-making and assertiveness are excepted from leaders, and unfortunately for educational contexts, differences are expected to be settled physically, by fighting. Some collectivist cultures are also extremely restrained and not inclined to indulgence. This is reflected in a lack of appreciation for leisure time or playtime and the suppression of the desires of individuals for the perceived common good of the group. While obviously mediated by the personal preferences of individuals, their belief systems, and values, some of these general characteristics are not easily accommodated in school contexts in individualist cultures and there is considerable responsibility on school leaders and staff to negotiate these differences from the initial contact on enrolment if necessary and to maintain informed communication and discussion as situations arise. While it is impossible to make people feel that they belong, it remains a prime indicator for social, emotional, and academic success.

Research findings

Developing effective transitions to school is vital to the eventual success of children and families with refugee backgrounds. For individuals who may not have felt seen, heard, or valued for many years and who bring fear and anxiety to new situations, arriving in a caring learning environment can have lasting positive implications. We spoke with an early childhood/primary principal in England and a preschool educator in Australia who offered ideas to support families and children in transition.

> *Context:* Our school serves pre-K to year six. Our leadership isn't hierarchical at all. Obviously there are decisions that I have to make, but my role is no less or no more valuable than anybody else's. We're all in it together. So we've done a lot of work on leadership and empowering people. But what I understand is that the role I play and the leadership team plays is absolutely critical. I have to walk the walk and talk the talk, this is what I call the moral imperative.

> At the admissions meeting, we find out lots of information from the parents about where they've come from, what their language is, what their religion

is. If there's anything the children don't need. But also we find out, and we ask about whether they are refugees or asylum seekers. whether they have leave to remain, whether they have recourse to public funds. So some of these are kind of awkward questions, and we wrangled about how we were going to introduce this. But our staff member she's brilliant. She really wants to know about the background, and she does it in a totally nonjudgmental way, because that's the most important thing, you know, is that we've got to be welcoming with people wherever they're from, whoever they are. We've got a smile and welcome.

We learned. We had a wonderful family who'd come from Nigeria. We didn't know a huge amount about the family. We didn't go into the detail that we currently do on our admissions process, so we didn't find out what their background was. But, it was around Christmas time, and Dad came in in floods of tears, saying that they were on the verge of being deported. We didn't know that they were asylum seekers, but I just kind of clicked into action because I do a lot of this kind of work as well, sending letters off to the authorities and it emerged that they were being deported because the solicitor had defaulted on a key piece of paperwork. Mom in Nigeria had been subjected to type 4 FGM (female genial mutilation) and she knew that if they were deported they'd be met at the airport by Nigerian community members who'd take the girls away and do exactly the same to them.

Context: We have 10% of our families identify as Aboriginal and Torres Strait Islanders and about 50% to 60% from culturally and linguistically diverse backgrounds, a small percentage of refugee families over the last few years. I am lucky enough to have a refugee support leader at my school. We have an onsite Department of Education preschool. We have a one-unit preschool, which provides 15 hours of preschool education per week to up to 20 children. But my school doesn't have capacity because we have a waiting list, and we're pretty full.

We were lucky that we had one teacher on a study tour down to Victoria a couple of years ago to look at the Kathy Walker programming in action. They are pioneers that started the shift in mindset, they were able to draw connections from play in the classroom to curriculum. Every teacher went 'we're not doing play over here, we're teaching English outcomes or maths or science outcomes over here.' It's just like seamlessly together. So, if we are looking at a science outcome, solids liquids easy for kids to go and play about, make some ice cubes, and watch the ice cubes melt in the sun because they want to do that, then it's the vocabulary. Incredible, the conversation that goes on around that in terms of deepening learning.

Treating these pre-schoolers like they're free-thinking, intelligent beings. It would be empowering for children from refugee and asylum seeker backgrounds because they're looking at other children the same age as them, actively participating in learning and risk-taking, risky play is okay. Things aren't going to go pear-shaped for them; it is worth taking a risk; grow in your self-confidence and self-motivation to want to go deeper. So, I love that, like the little girl last year, who didn't speak a word of English and was very introverted, has never left the mum's side, the carer's side within ten weeks of term, completely different child, absolutely different, confidence, smiling. She is eager, starting to articulate her wants and needs, and made some little friends to play with. She graduated. She started kindergarten. She's been really successful in the kindergarten classroom space. So, just that whole self-confidence, the little 4-year-olds, because I know that they can do anything. it does, that puts limitations on children.

Unique contexts, global principles

A consistent theme across our interviews and across this book has been the need to really know the young children and families with whom you are working. Our English principal had a near devastating experience with a newly arrived family that elevates the importance of knowing those you serve and changed the way her school operates. In this case, a bureaucratic error nearly caused a Nigerian family to be deported and the likely mutilation of two young girls. As a result, this school took a far more proactive and purposeful approach in the intake meetings with families, ensuring they use the time to develop trust but also gather extensive information about background, residency status, religion, and a host of other areas. This information combined with hiring and training a staff member to know government policies and practices has created a culture that truly can support families with refugee backgrounds. Our Australian preschool educator discussed her school's pedagogical approach that offers teachers, parents, and children an experience that is both academically rich and play-based in practice. By encouraging teachers to look at curriculum and instruction through the lens of play, this centre has created a space where children are joyous and well prepared for kindergarten, as evidenced by the story of the four-year old who blossomed.

Two themes that have emerged throughout this book are the power of play and the importance of knowing others. While these are certainly important values to espouse, they are little more than virtue-signalling if not combined with purposeful approaches. Our first research participant articulated the importance of a well-designed and comprehensive intake experience for new families. Our second participant offered a thoughtful pedagogical approach that clarified the notion of play-based learning. Across all contexts, well-meaning individuals need to be willing to reflect on what is and ask themselves if they have the knowledge to create the kind of environment they are seeking to develop. When the answer is uncertain, those who support our youngest and most vulnerable students need to seek understanding from researchers, colleagues, and the very people they are serving. As the five C's of Neoliberal

Education (Sellars & Imig, 2020a) have so strongly co-opted the ways education is organised and operated in many parts of the world, educators need to be willing to look beyond policies and expectations and ask 'what if?'

Conclusion

Ask almost any parent and you will discover the challenge of transitioning young children into new educational settings is very real and often full of anxiety. Combine a new educational setting with a new country, language, and culture and the importance of the transition process is magnified. Unfortunately, the ways children and families are often welcomed and integrated in preschools, day care centres, schools, and even playgroups are frequently shaped by Western expectations and practices that do not value the uniqueness of individuals or the values held by newly arrived families. As our research participants illustrated, educators have an opportunity to purposefully develop transition processes that both welcome and value new families and also gather information that will provide long-term support for those families. Further, rethinking programmes and policies with newly arrived families in mind can offer educators a fresh perspective to improve practice for all children.

References

Alder, M. (1993). The meaning of 'School ethos'. *Westminster Studies in Education,* *16,* 59–69.

Ball, S. (2016). Neoliberal education: Confronting the slouching beast. *Policy Futures in Education, 14*(8), 1–4. https://doi.org/10.1177/1478210316664259

Biesta, G. (2014). *The beautiful risk of education.* Paradigm Publishers.

Biesta, G., & Miedema, S. (2002). Instruction or pedagogy? The need for a transformative conception of education. *Teaching and Teacher Education, 18,* 173–181.

Bourdieu, P. (1986). The forms of capital. In J. G. Richardson (Ed.), *The handbook of theory: Research for the sociology of education* (pp. 241–258). Greenwood Press.

Bourdieu, P. (1990). *Reproduction in education, society, and culture.* Sage.

Bradley, M., & Sellars, M. (2021). Parent cafe reflections. In *Making a spectacle: Examining curriculum/pedagogy as recovery from political trauma* (pp. 183–189). Information Age Publishing.

Bragg, S. (2016). Perspectives on 'Choice and Challenge' in primary schools. *Improving Schools, 19*(1), 80–93. https://doi.org/10.1177/1365480216631079

Cacioppo, J. T., & Patrick, W. (2008). *Loneliness: Human nature and the need for social connection.* WW Norton & Company.

Chabot, S. 2008. "Love and Revolution." Critical Sociology 34 (6): 803–828. doi:10.1177/ 0896920508095100.

Coultas, V. (2015). Revisiting debates on oracy: Classroom talk: Moving towards a democratic pedagogy? *Changing English, 22*(1), 72–86. https://doi.org/10.1080/1358684x.2014.992205

Donnelly, C. (2000). In pursuit of school ethos. *British Journal of Educational Studies, 48*(2), 134–154.

Gary, K. (2016). Neoliberal education for work versus liberal education for leisure. *Studies in Philosophy and Education*, *36*(1), 83–94. https://doi.org/10.1007/s11217-016-9545-0

Gidley, J. (2016). *Postformal education: A philosophy for complex futures*. Springer.

Glover, D., & Coleman, M. (2005). School culture, climate and ethos: Interchangeable or distinctive concepts. *Journal of In-Service Education*, *31*(2), 251–272.

Hall, E. (1976). *Beyond culture*. Knopf Doubleday Publishing Group.

High, P. C., & AAP (American Academy of Pediatrics Committee on Early Childhood, Adoption, and Dependent Care and Council on School Health) (2008). School readiness. *Pediatrics*, *121*(4), e1008–1015. https://doi.org/10.1542/peds.2008-0079

Hofstede, G. (1986). Cultural differences in teaching and learning. *International Journal of Intercultural Relations*, *10*, 301–320.

Hofstede, G. (2001). *Culture's consequences: Comparing values, behaviors, institutions and organizations across nations* (2nd ed.). Sage.

Hofstede, G. (2011). Dimensionalizing cultures: The Hofstede model in context. *Online Readings in Psychology and Culture*, *2*, 1–26. https://doi.org/10.9707/2307-0919.1014

Hofstede, G., Hofstede, G. J., & Minkov, M. (2010). *Cultures and organisations: Software of the mind*. McGraw-Hill.

Kaukko, M., Wilkinson, J., & Kohli, R. (2021). Pedagogical love in Finland and Australia: A study of refugee children and their teachers. *Pedagogy, Culture & Society*, *30*, 1–17. https://doi.org/10.1080/14681366.2020.1868555

Lanas, M., & Zembylas, M. (2015). Revolutionary love at work in an arctic school with conflicts. *Teaching Education*, *26*(3), 272–287. https://doi.org/10.1080/10476210.2014.996744

Lewit, E. M., & Baker, L. S. (1995). School readiness. *The Future of Children*, *5*(2), 128. https://doi.org/10.2307/1602361

McLaughlin, T. (2005). The educative importance of ethos. *British Journal of Educational Studies*, *53*(3), 306–325. https://doi.org/10.1111/j.1467-8527.2005.00297.x

Mitchell, F., Gray, S., & Inchley, J. (2015). 'This choice thing really works…' Changes in experiences and engagement of adolescent girls in physical education classes, during a school-based physical activity programme. *Physical Education and Sport Pedagogy*, *20*(6), 593–611. https://doi.org/10.1080/17408989.2013.837433

Minkov, M., Bond, M. H., Dutt, P., Schachner, M., Morales, O., Sanchez, C., Jandosova, J., Khassenbekov, Y., & Mudd, B. (2017). A reconsideration of Hofstede's fifth dimension: New flexibility versus monumentalism data from 54 countries. *Cross-Cultural Research*, *52*(3), 309–333. https://doi.org/10.1177/1069397117727488

Pan, Q., Trang, K. T., Love, H. R., & Templin, J. (2019). School readiness profiles and growth in academic achievement. *Frontiers in Education*, *4*. https://doi.org/10.3389/feduc.2019.00127

Potmesilova, P., & Potmesil, M. (2021). Temperament and school readiness: A literature review. *Frontiers in Psychology*, *12*, 599411. https://doi.org/10.3389/fpsyg.2021.599411

Rock, D. (2008). SCARF: A brain-based model for collaborating with and influencing others. *NeuroLeadership Journal*, *1*, 1–9.

Rock, D., & Cox, C. (2012). SCARF® in 2012: Updating the social neuroscience of collaborating with others. *NeuroLeadership Journal, 4,* 1–14. Retrieved February 24, 2020, from https://pdfs.semanticscholar.org/5f7b/37514e26877f8e0c1c156 c1009f8e9970d7a.pdf

Rosa, M., & Orey, D. C. (2015). A trivium curriculum for mathematics based on literacy, matheracy, and technoracy: An ethnomathematics perspective. *ZDM, 47*(4), 587–598. https://doi.org/10.1007/s11858-015-0688-1

Sellars, M. (2008). *Using students' strengths to support learning outcomes: A study of the development of Gardner's intrapersonal intelligence to support increased academic achievement for primary school students.* VDM Verlag.

Sellars, M. (2014). *Reflective practice for teachers* (1st ed.). Sage.

Sellars, M. (2020). *Educating students with refugee and asylum seeker experiences: A commitment to humanity.* Verlag Barbara Budrich.

Sellars, M. (2021). Belonging and being: Developing inclusive ethos. *International Journal of Leadership in Education,* 1–24. https://doi.org/10.1080/13603124.2 021.1942994

Sellars, M., & Imig, S. (2020a). The real cost of neoliberalism for educators and students. *International Journal of Leadership in Education, 26,* 1–13. https://doi.org/ 10.1080/13603124.2020.1823488

Sellars, M., & Imig, D. (2020b). Pestalozzi and pedagogies of love: Pathways to educational reform. *Early Child Development and Care, 191,* 1152–1163. https:// doi.org/10.1080/03004430.2020.1845667

Shahjahan, R. A. (2011). Decolonizing the evidence-based education and policy movement: Revealing the colonial vestiges in educational policy, research, and neoliberal reform. *Journal of Education Policy, 26*(2), 181–206. https://doi.org/10.1080/0 2680939.2010.508176

Solvason, C. (2005). Investigating specialist school ethos......or do you mean culture? *Educational Studies, 31*(1), 85–94.

Williams, P. G., et al. (2019). School readiness. *Pediatrics, 144*(2). https://doi. org/10.1542/peds.2019-1766

Zheyu, L., Weijin, C., Jihui, Z., Yuan, W., Ghani, U., & Zhai, X. (2021). Investigating the influence of tacit knowledge transformation approach on students' learning ability. *Frontiers in Psychology, 12,* 647729. https://doi.org/10.3389/ fpsyg.2021.647729

Chapter 9

Putting the research together

Perspectives, challenges, and opportunities

Introduction

The prior eight chapters offered research findings from more than 30 educators working in a variety of settings (playgroups, preschools, day care centres, and primary schools) and countries (Australia, England, New Zealand, Northern Ireland, and the United States). In each setting, the participants brought their own knowledge, experience, and beliefs to their daily work with their unique students and under their unique policy requirements. The findings from these participants offer numerous examples of good practice and confronting insights about the challenge of effectively meeting the needs of children and family with refugee and asylum-seeker backgrounds. In this final chapter, the authors offer their perspectives on the major findings from the research that comprised this volume. This chapter includes three conversations held by the authors, each framed around one of the book's major themes: (i) trauma and intergenerational trauma, (ii) social and emotional development, notions of childhood, and transitioning to school, and (iii) inclusion. The conversations capture the authors' perspectives on the complex work undertaken by these early childcare practitioners. And, just as the many participants who offered insights for this book didn't share uniformly consistent opinions about effective practices and policies, the authors offer differing perspectives on the meaning and importance of the research presented. Readers are encouraged to glean insights that may be applicable from these conversations to their own contexts.

This chapter summarises some of the major complexities and challenges that the research participants articulated in their responses. These were broadly identified using three major themes: *culture, context,* and *trauma.* The conversations that follow are the authors' discussions of the ways in which they perceived some of the challenges and complexities of the work undertaken by these early childcare practitioners in the course of their daily work. The chapter themes were grouped into associated aspects of the work undertaken and the discussions were led in turn by each author. These conversations are intended to provide a less formal, more intimate perspective of the researchers'

DOI: 10.4324/9781003404231-10

interests and reflections on their experiences and pedagogical beliefs about this early childhood educational and caring context and they express the foundational value and importance they place on these critical stages of development in the lives of children with refugee and asylum-seeker experiences. It also seeks to acknowledge the individuals who undertake to support these processes positively, with empathy and sensitivity, accepting that many points of difference enrich their work and encourages them to think and work creatively. While there are many diverse ways of looking at the world and how best to interact with the different cultural expectations that these present, especially within collectivist and individualist cultures, the research participants remained sensitive to the particular needs of individual children and their families, understanding that cultural differences may be general but also specific, and all societies are composed of individuals and groups who have particular strengths, requirements, and beliefs to help them navigate their new homelands and its expectations.

Conversation: trauma and intergenerational trauma

SI: Trauma is something that has been front and centre in so many of our conversations. As we talk about the forced displacement and loss and about the real trauma these families have experienced, I think sometimes the words can begin to lose their weight. I was hoping we could talk about trauma and what we heard in our interviews. Were there moments where you said to yourself, *this is really important, and this research needs to happen?* I thought that might be a good jumping off point to set the stage that we're dealing with some big issues here.

MS: I think one of our participants mentioned they had a family come in and someone was talking to them, saying, 'Everything will be fine.' And one of the participants said this family couldn't talk about what they'd been through, or how they felt because of the social stigma of mental health. And that is something that is critical to how all of this is dealt with in terms of people being able to talk about how they feel, being able to not feel ashamed of the ways in which they don't cope now, compared to the ways in which they used to. Being able to accept that culturally, mental health is viewed very differently in their new homeland.

So, I think stigma around it is a very big deal in terms of the parents' capacities to recover from and then to not pass on the intergenerational trauma impact to their children. So that to me is something that's critical in this work. In other work I've done around parents, especially mothers, they seem to be left to deal with a lot of trauma by themselves. Not that the males in the family are not traumatised or not impacted but may be in different ways, so there may even be a gendered type of response to trauma.

DI: I would only add that I think when we talk about adverse childhood experiences, we talk about frequency of exposure, duration of exposure, and then protective factors that can protect against that exposure. I think so many of the family experiences shared through our interviews suggest all the ways in which resilience can break down over time. The principal who said, 'Put yourself in the position of some of these families who in effect are prisoners. They have no control over where they live. They have no control over their lives right now. They must have their kids in out-of-home care because they have to be in English class and the clock is ticking. They only have this kind of support for a certain number of days.' It's a lot.

SI: I think you both make wonderful points. At the most concrete level, I remember educators who told us about the lights going off in the classroom and children screaming and crying, because when the lights go off it means there's danger. And the loud noise on the road, they talked about when a car drives by, and it might have a backfire, the kids diving under tables. Just the fact these children equate sounds and those experiences with horrible memories is, you know, it's such a stark reminder of what these children have gone through.

Maura, you brought up a point about intergenerational trauma. There is this reality that a lot of these children may not have personally seen the violence or experienced the loss the parents have, because either they were born in their host country. So, they grow up in homes where they're experiencing trauma through their parents. I'm curious about that. What did we learn from our educators that would be valuable in terms of dealing with children experiencing intergenerational trauma?

MS: I think one of the things we have to remember here is all the information that's coming to light at the moment about the genetic modification of the biological processes in the womb, about all of that being changed by these huge amounts of cortisol which are actually blocking some of the other hormones and some of the other processes. I think all that *in utero* that is being passed on is something we need to remember now that didn't necessarily come from our participants, because that's well outside of their range of expertise, perhaps. But they do see the impact. And I think one of the things I find challenging is one of our participants did say two of the children in a family were born in refugee camps. So, they were born into trauma and it's more obvious trauma. But there's a lot of trauma that would have been happening much less explicitly, sort of within the womb, within the nurturing process.

The other thing is that we look at violence and bombing and fleeing and displacement, losing loved ones, grief, all those as traumatic events, and we forget sometimes that living in poverty, that inadequate security and shelter and housing, and all those things are equally traumatic for families. So it could be that some of these families have always suffered from a great deal of trauma. Maybe it became more acceptable because they weren't the only people in those communities living like that. But in many ways, there is trauma from all directions, and we're talking about complex childhood trauma like Doug said in terms of frequency, in terms of duration, but also in terms of different sources if you like. Different reasons to be traumatised, and that becomes a huge load. And so, I think for parents to sort of bear the brunt of all those things and know that it's impacting on their lives, they're forced to flee, be displaced, then they're in transit, and they're traumatised again. Then they arrive in a new homeland if they're fortunate. But, like somebody said, it's like winning a golden ticket. But, it's another round of trauma for many families.

DI: Scott, I wanted to add a reflection on some of the points that Maura was sharing, which I think are so important. I am reminded of the story shared by one of our respondents of Frank, the little boy from El Salvador who presented in his preschool classroom as a behavior issue, that he couldn't sit still. He was acting out. In a stroke of brilliance, the teacher asked the children to do a self-portrait and this child did a portrait of a man with his face covered and another man with his hands up, and explained that this was a *bandolero*, and he had killed his grandfather. It's a powerful and important story and it's haunting. While the child had not seen this murder himself, his mother confirmed that this happened, and it was why they had to leave El Salvador. I think this is a telling example of how something that happened to a previous generation has very much shaped this child's self-perception. It was telling that the instructor said, from that point on little Frank went from being a 'behavior problem' to being a child that had lived through and suffered through all these things. The teacher went on to say, 'it makes us wonder how many more Franks are there in the classroom.' I think that's an incredibly important realisation.

SI: This is an idea we heard from several participants who talked about not conflating behaviours related to trauma with, say, learning difficulties. I remember we had an educator from the Midwest in the United States who said we need to be mindful not to label these students at an early age.

MS: I was just going to say that having noted many of these people lived in poverty and had difficult lives before they were displaced, they also have a degree of strength and resilience. So, one of the things we have to be very sensitive to is not pathologising the trauma. I don't think it's our job to do that. It was very interesting for me to review and reflect on our participants, some of whom said knowing as much as we can helps us, and I thought that's a very valid point. Then other participants say we haven't asked, if we're not told, we don't ask. We work with what we find out. We work with what we know, even though it's very, very little. I think there's a very fine line here always between allowing some autonomy in a world where these communities have very little control over their lives. Allowing them to the masters of something in their lives. It's at this stage when they're settling in, and when they first arrive, because, as we noted before, they have no say where they live, what sort of conditions they live, in which neighbourhoods they end up. So, there's a fine line between pathologising the trauma and being supportive, generous, and intuitively sensitive; just understanding that it is a personal decision to discuss their circumstances or not.

DI: Scott, you had asked previously about the clash of cultures or the juxtaposition of cultures which may not be aligned around some of these issues. Can you speak to that just a little bit more? Are you thinking in terms of reactions to trauma or understandings of family backgrounds?

SI: We have discussed the idea that trauma doesn't end when somebody arrives in a new country. In fact, it continues for many people and part of that is because you arrive in a new land, where not only you do not speak the language but your ways of being are also so different from your peers. We heard from an educator who said, 'I have Arab parents saying, I want my child to eat with their right hand. Don't let him eat with his left,' even though the child is left-handed. It's challenging, it is cultural conflicts. For a family that's arriving and doesn't have a network of friends, this furthers the stress and anxiety they're feeling. It furthers trauma. I wonder if there were anecdotes from our educators with insights about how to address this clash of cultures?

MS: In the introduction we were talking about the clash of cultures, the big differences between collectivist and individualist cultures, as Hofstede would call them. I think that a lot of what is left unsaid, that we take for granted about the ways of doing and being, and the sorts of things we believe are important are those things that are causing the most trauma in culture. Things like the toileting issue of these little boys are intensely personal and private. Nobody would question: 'Do your children know how to use a Western style toilet?' It's not what you would ask in an interview for a preschool, or when you're getting to know the parents. I think a lot of the difficulties lie in the unconscious way in which we do personal and private things and the attitudes and values that we bring to that. I think that's where we're getting big clashes of uncertainty and misunderstandings. We need to see things from a different perspective. Because it's not something that culturally we belong to and so we have to put ourselves out of our comfort zone to actually even consider those things. I think the participants who brought those stories to us really recognised what is essentially critical for a lot of these families may not be the big things like curriculum, and what the children do, or you know the fact maybe they have two languages interspersed together, and don't speak one or the other purely in its original form. I think it's things that are private and personal and important.

DI: I absolutely agree with Maura. Our respondents made it clear that giving children and their families a sense of safety and security is essential to moving forward. There can be no curriculum-based learning without the foundation of trust and safety. There is reason to be optimistic here: the educators we interviewed made it clear they are willing to bend, they recognise that traditional ways of doing things don't make sense with cohorts of kids from other backgrounds. Maybe we used to have tables and chairs in the classroom, but our children now aren't familiar with Western style chairs. So now we have carpets. We have places where mom can come in if she wants to privately change a nappy on her own. This isn't something that necessarily she has to entrust to a stranger. Maura reminds us of the brothers who had special water bottles for toileting, which were difficult for the teacher to understand. I love the solution in that particular case where the family and the school agreed the boys could use wet wipes. Finding flexibility, allowing a level of autonomy, finding space for compromise: these are gifts, and they are difficult in a setting where people are trying very hard to meet the needs of classrooms full of children. I think we encountered many of those stories in this research.

MS: I think one of the most commendable things that I find in the stories our participants shared with us was in a very highly regulated environment they find some flexibility. They find room to make things work. Because, apart from their own capacity to be sensitive, to have empathy, to be knowledgeable, and to anticipate what some of these people may find threatening, they are also accountable, if you like, to the authorities that governed the institution. This is what these people have brought us, these amazing juggling acts that are done with kindness and generosity. And that's why we can have hope because we have people like these scattered throughout the world.

SI: One of the things we've discovered in doing this kind of research for years is our participants seem to do an incredible job of advocating for families and pushing up against policy. They seem to be almost policy entrepreneurs in that they can look at policy and say, 'How do I make that work for me? How do I make that work in my setting?' We heard from the educator in England who talked about going on the radio and television to advocate for families. We heard from an Irish educator pushing back against community racism and being vocal that it's not acceptable to talk about newly arrived families this way. I think you're right that what draws people to this work is something inherent in them. They care.

Another thing that came up in our research repeatedly is that these educators are so underpaid and so poorly funded by society. Many directors told us they can't keep their staff because they can go down the street to Walmart and get a better paying job. So how do people who are reading this book create wonderful organisations for young learners? How can they infuse passion in their staff? What did you hear from our participants about creating organisations with excellent teams?

MS: I think there are a number of things that come up here. Firstly, I don't think it's infused, I think it's there. I think it's ready to be ignited. To choose a job in early childhood education takes particular types of people. There is something intrinsically human about these sorts of wonderful people who face this day after day. And, as much as I agree it's a leadership thing, it's also one of those things where I believe you can't make a team work successfully unless you have a common agenda, a common goal, and a common vision for your work. The people who work together must find particular types of educators for these situations. You have to step back and think they're just amazing human beings. They may be inspired by the leadership, but they've got to have what it takes really in terms of their own motivations, their own innate human capacities for compassion and authentic empathy.

DI: Scott, you're raising a really important and difficult question here. To Maura's point, it has to be about more than the money, and particularly in some of our national contexts where pay is so far below a living wage. The other place I go in thinking about your question is, in effect, how do we fundamentally shift the public conception of early childhood education from glorified babysitting to a foundational need for early childhood development, school readiness, and the maintenance of a workforce.

MS: A lot of early childcare workers are undervalued, and the work they do is so critical. Everybody would agree that the first five years of life are a time of accelerated development. It's the time of setting all sorts of foundations for life. For children who may have experienced high levels of trauma, compounded by underlying cultural differences in their families of origin, we're asking them to live a dual existence in some ways. So, I agree with what you said earlier that we need to learn to compromise, because what we're after is integration, and integrating large communities of traumatised people into any society is not going to be an easy job for generations to come.

SI: I think this is a nice place to wrap up this conversation. We have come from the roots of trauma, how it manifests itself in school, all the way through what we need to do societally to begin addressing these big picture issues that will benefit all children. I appreciate how both of you engaged with this.

Conversation: social and emotional development, notions of childhood, and transitioning to school

DI: Today, let's talk about social and emotional learning, the role of play, and transitions from birth through early childhood and into later life. Let's begin with Piaget's observation that 'play is the work of children.' Through play, through interacting with the world around them, children learn, grow, and develop. This process is particularly critical in early childhood when millions of synaptic connections are forming every second.

Were there certain anecdotes shared by our respondents that shed light on the importance of developing the capacity to play, the capacity to interact with the world in safe ways, particularly for young children in families with refugee and asylee experiences?

MS: I think we are very 'Piagetian' in the Western world in terms of thinking about childhood. And I think that the notion of play being children's work doesn't necessarily gel with Asian parents, maybe Confucian-based societies. They prefer to think perhaps that as they are culturally disciplined, the disciplined minds that their very young children are encouraged to develop, that children are more fruitfully served by beginning to engage with what is given to them in the form of information, knowledge, and processes by the adults. So, in other words, they're better off being directly taught. So, I think that this is where this sort of notion of a cultural clash becomes quite apparent.

SI: The interesting thing we heard from nearly all respondents was the importance and fundamental nature of play in the work they do. We heard from multiple educators who talked about the value of risky play, about taking children out and playing by creeks and swinging on ropes and building forts, and the value of that for building connections to place and people is vital. This goes back to the importance of experience before explicit instruction. This type of play gives children shared experiences and a shared language they can bring back to the classroom with them.

MS: As a teacher, my mantra was always 'experience before explicit,' I do think that what was reflected in our participants' stories was some resistance to this notion of play. If you want children's work, then what you give them in some societies is responsibility. They look after the other children, they chop things and prepare meals, they bring in the wood for fires. If you introduce Piaget's notion that play is children's work in these societies, they'll say, well, this is children's work.

DI: One of the threads that surfaced in many of our conversations was that some children with refugee experiences have a 'play deficit.' They don't know how to interact with the world around them through play. Were strategies shared by our respondents that you found particularly inspiring in encouraging play-based interaction?

SI: One of my favourite examples was the simple story of the playgroup in New Zealand bringing in the mothers and the young children and having them sit across from each other and rolling a ball back and forth. Simply understanding that that type of 'serve and return' interaction counts as play. It was two generations in that example who had never learned how to play. Then to hear an Australian preschool teacher talk about giving mothers and children language to talk about play. The power of that was tremendous. Teaching mothers to build a tower with their child and then how to talk to them. 'Wow, it's getting taller. Look, we're making it higher. Oh, look! It may fall.' Helping families realise play is important, it's foundational and then also giving them language around it was incredibly important.

MS: Even strategies like having the bus pick up the mothers and bring them to playgroup, so it was an interactive, a participatory sort of activity as well as setting up the play buddies. One of our respondents talked about the play buddies, and I think that this is one aspect that probably those who are not in favour or don't see the value of children's play do not recognise. I think there are several things happening within that sort of community who don't necessarily see that children's play is supportive of cognitive development, and it is important. I think that play very often, especially for children of a certain age, preschool children for example, may be violent, and would be playing out, maybe what they have nightmares about, what they have seen, what they're afraid of. So, it would have a very negative connotation in many ways in that it was interaction, but it was aggressive. It had the possibility of becoming violent. That's something, I think, that a lot of even older children – six, seven, eight year olds – would bring to their artwork and their interactions with other children. So, it's the sort of social and emotional development that we would be thinking may be good for them psychologically, but it's not that good for them, socially and emotionally. Also, I think that in collectivist societies, very much of the interaction is predestined. Social and emotional development, and cognition are seen as certain types of behaviours which are compliant and obedient, and the cognition is gaining information and gaining knowledge from the adults, because the adults are the role-makers for their children and their behaviours.

And so, the social and emotional complexities and skills that we can gain from engaging children in play, and even the knowledge may not be as necessary. Collective societies may not see that as necessary, because it's also predestined but it may be more an individualistic societal need because in collective societies you are naturally and physically related and connected to groups. And so many refugee and asylum-seeking communities seek the group that fits with their notion of being connected. I'm just wondering whether this social and emotional development that we talk about is critical, and I certainly believe it is.

DI: Maura, thank you for that wonderful segue to the connection between social and emotional learning and cognitive development. In many Western societies, we focus on cognitive skills. We measure students' achievement in terms of math and literacy success. Yet early childhood educators have resisted that push, and instead have understood social and emotional learning as intimately bound up with cognitive development. Can you think of examples shared by our respondents of a disconnect between social and emotional learning, and cognitive development?

MS: I think more than one of the respondents said that they have families who come and feel that play is a waste of time. The other thing is that you know, I think when you've lost everything and you're looking at education as a way of regaining something in life for your children, status, security, emotional stability. Then it's almost like they want their children started on that path now, so that they are able to be successful in educational terms because that's their pathway to building a new life for themselves. So, I think when the early years educators were talking about different parents who'd come and not really understood the importance of play or said that they felt that they lost parents because they were play based. That they were just highlighting for us, that our presumption of play-based education is not automatically shared and I think the main disconnect that we heard in the research was the parents who maybe diminish the value of play.

SI: Sometimes we forget who these folks are. We can assume because they're refugees, maybe they themselves came from poverty, and they were uneducated. But many of these folks who come were professionals in their home countries and they recognise that education, more than anything else, is going to be the key to help the next generation of their family. I think one tension these preschool professionals are facing is parents who are saying, 'Look, we have a tight window of time here to get the next generation on their feet.' But fortunately, we spoke with 30 plus educators around the world who get that. And these educators were able to help families understand the value of play, and the value of social, emotional learning.

MS: There was a nice little story about an educator who was doing play-based therapy, and she was doing that with children, and involving parents, too. But it was mostly aimed at the child, and I think that she was saying that they see great benefit from play-based therapy and I can imagine that socially and emotionally that that would be something critical for a lot of these children. That play would be the therapy, apart from the interaction, the social, emotional, or whatever. I think that even the violent play enacted in a relatively safe and monitored environment would probably reassure some of them and make them feel much more comfortable about their experiences as play-based therapy.

DI: Let's talk for a minute about the relationship between trauma and learning. A number of our respondents underscored the primary need to establish conditions of trust and safety, both physical and psychological safety, before anything else can happen. Remember the one educator who said that her newest children with refugee experiences would run to the snack table and put all the snacks in their pockets. She would simply explain to the other children that the new children need to do this until they realise the snacks come back every day. They don't need to hoard them anymore. And that's fine. Just let them.

Perhaps that anecdote suggests the foundational nature of safety and security before early childhood learning and development can take place. Were there parallel examples that resonated with you where our respondents had worked to establish those conditions of safety that allowed their children and families to move forward on their developmental pathways?

SI: We heard repeatedly about the need to be proactive. Your example of the granola bars is powerful. In Maslow's physiological needs, that's foundational. But the other thoughtful thing the educator in that case did was talk to the other students and help them understand. The thing we heard from a lot of educators was the need to be proactive in terms of scanning the environment, constantly figuring out what are the causes, what are the triggers for anxiety. The preschool director who told us her centre is on a busy road. Cars drive by, sometimes cars make loud noises and that equates to fear for some children. So, she spends time helping them understand that cars can make loud noises. She couldn't control the fire alarms, so she brought in the custodian from the building and had the custodian set off a fire alarm after she had explained to the students that it was going to happen. She explained what it means. This is a test. Educators need to constantly be proactive.

MS: And I think what we know now is that many of the people who are coming here are coming for political reasons, perhaps they were in high-status professions, perhaps they made powerful political enemies. In addition, a huge number of people are undereducated for a technological world. The technological society that they're coming into can be overwhelming. But it's also allowed us to understand how trauma impacts on cognition and how the build-up of the cortisol and all of what happens in the brain can delete or delay the development of other processes that are critical to effective thinking at any age or stage. The first three years, and the first five years of life in particular, are very important in setting the scene for learning and the capacity to learn at certain levels before neural pruning that occurs when they're about five or coming into six, depending on their developmental timeline. I think that much of this negative impact has to be somehow resolved and the children supported so that they can develop their cognitive capacities positively, whether it's through play therapy or whether it's through play, whether it's through secure environments, whether it's through bringing the mothers in giving the children a sense of security. One of our Australian educators said, 'You know that children won't mix. They hang on to their mother's legs.' They're hanging on to the only security they know, because everything else is just so unpredictable that you know this sense of being able to develop as an individual, even at a very young age, is very inhibited. If we don't have play, even though people feel it's a waste of time, where do we get supportive opportunities for the chemical balances to rebalance themselves and allow all of these synapses and allow all of these parts of the brain that can and will coordinate with each other and work well. Young children learn by interacting with the people and places in their lives. If we don't encourage that through play, how can we?

DI: Maura, I think you're highlighting one of the themes that runs throughout the volume, which is the underlying tension between what is culturally constructed and what is universal across all societies and all places. When we speak of the science of early brain development, for example, we act as if brain development occurs in a consistent way across all children. At the same time, we also say that development will happen differently in different contexts, and it can be thwarted by negative experiences, and then resilience needs to be built.

Were there vignettes shared in this research that highlight the ways that conceptions of childhood are culturally constructed, or ways in which early childhood development is a universal process, and that all children develop in parallel ways and consequently deserve to be raised, prioritised, and valued in a certain way?

MS: I liked the educator who said, you can't just teach. You know they need to play. We're not teaching them anything explicitly at the moment, we are not going to do anything with them at the moment, and they're in a preschool environment, they need to play, play, play. Also, one of the educators highlighted the degree of control if you like. That some parents have been overzealous about keeping their children safe almost to the point of isolating them in their own little cultural world. They need to learn to tie their shoelaces or their buckles, or whatever, because when they go to big school, nobody's going to do it for them. That's part of the notion of keeping the children dependent on adults to reinforce this sense of community and belonging, and everybody needing each other and for me that speaks to the social and emotional. But it also speaks to the cognitive. When I read things about keeping children close to you, helping with their toileting, even things like that, I keep thinking, when will this child have independence? Maybe because I'm from an individualistic society, I'm thinking, when is this child experiencing, exploring for themselves?

SI: I think a lot of these cultural differences we have to recognise are also being looked at through the lens of trauma. So, it's exacerbating some of these factors that Maura talked about. You know this collectivism versus individualism. You know that we heard from directors talking about the fact that the parents are hand-feeding their children when they're three to four years old. We heard about parents who don't want their 18 year olds to move out because they're not ready. They need to stay for many, many more years. That's a product of culture. But it's also a product of culture seen through the prism of the trauma that they've experienced. I think we need to keep that in mind.

MS: Yes and no. I think that the trauma probably exacerbated those feelings of keeping people close and not encouraging them to be so independent. I suppose my thinking is how do they fare? How in the future will they be included? How in the future are they going to work in an individualistic society? We're getting again to this fine line of how do we blend two cultures?

DI: Let's unpack that a little bit more. Were there ways in which our educators talked of creating a kind of inclusion which is a blending of cultures and other ways in which they instead drew hard lines between what is acceptable and what is not?

SI: Both. Yes, I think the message we heard throughout is it comes down to being thoughtful and reflective. I think we heard that repeatedly from our participants in terms of doing things purposefully. Being careful about helping children feel like they have a connection in your organisation, in the playgroup, in the preschool, and at the day care centre. It's having familiar things. It's having cultural events and flags and books and foods. But it's also being incredibly mindful of not being tokenistic. And so, it's really walking that fine line. And that's why I say, you have to be thoughtful and reflective, because what we discovered from our participants was, look, you try something and you pull back if it's not working, and you do more of it if it is working. This is a job that requires people to be incredibly attentive to the work.

MS: I think what you spoke about earlier, Scott was very powerful as well. As an educator, you spend your life scanning, not just looking for triggers, but scanning, scanning for possibilities, scanning for triggers, scanning for probabilities. And I think that it's something that requires a great deal of attentiveness, a great deal of living in the moment and being aware of the moment. We are saying now that we want these children to grow up to acknowledge, understand, and work with the traditions of their first culture, but we also want them to be able to operate in a different world as well. When we're actually encouraging and supporting all of this play-based learning, different ways of doing, different ways of knowing, using what technology has taught us about how the brain works and how we work as people, what we're doing is to create, hopefully, a new, less divided society. But in order to do that, our practices in education are one of those huge influences on children and societies. So, we're asking our educators very much through our work to work with children so that they can understand, and their families understand and accept a different way of knowing and doing, but also keep enough of their original identities to be authentic.

DI: Let me use that observation to tee up a final question: Do our findings in this research underscore key ways to understand social and emotional learning for children with traumatic and refugee experiences and backgrounds? And if we were to push ourselves further, do our findings suggest ways to upgrade and strengthen the literature on social and emotional learning for children in families with refugee experiences?

MS: Yes. It's the stress on social and emotional learning, because people are social beings, and it's also developing the capacity for *salutogenesis* which is primarily how people manage to lead happy and satisfied lives and I don't mean happy, as in partying, I mean contented lives and lives where they feel that they contribute. But they're also acknowledged for themselves that they're not subsumed into a larger sort of collaborative society, in which they are sort of a worker bee. What we're learning from the research is that people are coming with different ideas about how traumatised children need to be and need to be treated. Many of these societies don't necessarily recognise trauma.

SI: Maura, I think you hit on something really important. If you look at the standards for teachers around the world, if you look here in Australia, you'll see trauma doesn't make an appearance and that's a problem. When we talk about the key takeaways from all this work, the importance of understanding trauma and understanding social emotional development for children are central. There is this Foucauldian notion that society and schools are mirrors of each other. Schools develop societies and vice versa. I think what we need to do at this point is start learning from the experts to inform society, and the experts are the preschool teachers, the early childhood centre directors, the playgroup directors. I think we need to use their insights.

Conversation: Inclusion

The entire purpose of this work revolves around the notion of authentic inclusion, how can it be established for newcomers whose lives have been severely disrupted and who are facing a future in a homeland with very different lifestyles, expectations, and beliefs to many of their own. What does inclusion entail?

MS: It's not uncommon to hear educators say, 'oh yes, we have included everyone' and encourage all the children to join in whatever activity has been planned, irrespective of the nature of the activity. This may lead to clashes of well held beliefs, such as the disapproval of some Islamic groups of engaging in musical activities and dancing in contexts other than religious. Given the cultural diversity and contextual variance we found in our research, what do you think constitutes authentic inclusion?

Did you find anything in our participants' responses that would indicate how they interpreted authentic inclusion in their contexts?

SI: I think what I've pulled from our interviews is that it is basically the acknowledgement and acceptance of the whole person. It's the acceptance and appreciation of language, of dress, of food, of customs. It's also understanding that people are more than those things. They're also shaped by their experiences, and they're shaped by the lives they had before they arrived in these new settings. We've spent a lot of time talking about trauma, but, when we think about these families, we need to remember they bring a lot more than just those traumatic experiences.

DI: Scott, I appreciate your effort to clear some definitional underbrush. We are using terms like *assimilation, integration, inclusion,* and *belonging* in specific ways and we owe our reader a little bit of context for these. I think the Early Childhood Educators we spoke with, as a group, attempt to respect the cultures of their families, and at the same time, they also want to be sure that those families understood the boundaries of the law in their new host societies. Our respondents shared that they try to clarify the limits on corporal punishment, for example, while trying not to pass judgement on things that might be culturally specific. 'We focus on making sure that new families understand the laws in their new home.' We also had quite a number of respondents who were very interested in helping families find ways that were comfortable for them to engage with each other, and also to celebrate their home festivals and to encourage community linkages among families who might share a culture of origin. We had a respondent who talked about celebrating Eid at the conclusion of Ramadan. And yet, they did so in a way that did not focus on the religious dimension of the celebration. In the same way, they celebrated the secular aspects of Easter. And yet that is a difficult line to walk: when you try to separate out the candy and the coloured eggs from the 'other' Easter story. But I think we would all applaud the effort, to the extent possible, to acknowledge that there are cultural differences, and we can come together to celebrate them.

MS: So given that these are the sorts of things that participants are saying, were any particular examples you found where you feel that people made big efforts to acknowledge difference. Different ways of doing and knowing and celebrating?

SI: I think this book is infused with that. I think that's foundational to almost everything. One of my favourite examples was the playgroup director who talked about having each of the mothers bring their culture to the playgroup and talk about their culture and their values and their foods and their dress, and every aspect of it. She said you can also talk about your religion as well, but the only rule is, nothing shared can make anybody else in the group feel like they're not valued, or they don't belong. I think that's the idea. I think that's what authentic inclusion looks like.

MS: It's very important to have an acceptance. You talked about a number of things there. But if we look at Hall's cultural iceberg, we find it's those hidden things. It's the attitude and perspectives. And of course, Hall is all about interpersonal relationships and interpersonal relationships on that iceberg, so the surface stuff of the food and the clothes and the music and things which are interesting and valuable. But it's the attitudes and values that other people need to respect. For those people presenting differences in culture. They need to not make others feel that they are minimising others by commenting on their particular choices. So, I think that that speaks a lot towards what we feel authentic inclusion can be, because it's that negotiated acceptance. Without any negativity, negative under- or overtones about what is valued and what isn't, because we need to value it all.

MS: What do you understand is the relationship, if any, between inclusion and integration? And essentially between inclusion and belonging? What do you feel would be/should be priority concern when planning for inclusion? Did our participants share anything in their stories that made you reconsider what constitutes authentic inclusion, who determines what inclusive practices may look like or the complexities of planning inclusive practices for children with diverse backgrounds and home lives?

SI: You talk about the difficulty of this work. I think for the people that we spoke with, and for the people who will be reading this book, I think it's simple for them. It's the work they do. I think, for those of us who try to conceptualise it and capture it as researchers. I think that's where the complexity comes in. Sometimes when you try to lay a framework or a taxonomy over people's behaviours, that's the tricky work. But the people who are reading this, they are the ones who do it.

MS: I would agree with that. But there's a lot of thinking and a lot of sensitivity that goes into things like activities. What book to read? Which books are more inclusive of different ideas than others? Selecting a storybook for children is not simple. The simplest book can have enormously beneficial undertones and overtones for some of these children, if we think deeply enough about it. In terms of those sorts of activities, I think these people might find it simple, but I think it's they find it simple because they're so good at it, and they're so tuned in.

SI: Well, just to clarify. The people who do this work every day are really good at reading and responding and reflecting. And so, when I say it's simple, it's experience. It's because these educators are in tune with their students and their families. They can try something, quickly recognise if it's working or not, and they can modify practice. We would be silly to think that anybody has the answers to all this figured out. That's a huge piece of this is, coming into all this work with this understanding that everybody is learning how to do this work well.

MS: I think so, but I also think that there's an enormous amount of learning. Not just a reflection and going with your instinct. There's an enormous amount of theoretical learning and philosophy about what is best for child development. And in the way in which our resources are provided and how we present them. It's like, you know, making the maracas with rice or painting with pasta when you've got people who have been in the past extremely short of food. So, I take your point about reflecting on their families and communities. It's about choosing things that are not just innocuous, but choosing things like these stories that allow children to be themselves, because being different can be very difficult. So, in this inclusive practice, I would like to cite your earlier conversation, and the example that you gave about the mothers. This example of inclusion was that no one else can feel belittled by what we do. I think this is the enormously philosophical and theoretical background to what these people do that makes it look simple. I think they're incredibly thoughtful and reflective and well educated and much underrated for the extremely sensitive work they do.

MS: What do you think are the challenges in individualistic cultures (such as those experienced in the new homelands of many families of refugee and asylum-seeker backgrounds) of promoting inclusion and belonging for newcomers with backgrounds in collectivist societies? Were there narratives in the participants responses that alerted you to some of these challenges? What do you think are the challenges in individualistic cultures. such as the ones in which our communities have been placed as a result of their displacement from their own countries?

DI: One of the historical foundations for the kindergarten and the nursery school movements, at least in the United States, was as a way to socialise the children of immigrants into a new society. It was an effort to make sure that children of parents with political views that were considered potentially dangerous were properly socialised to be good Americans. And so that socialisation function is a key reason why Western societies do have preschool and nursery school.

Our respondents made it clear that they are trying to do many different things all at once. They are trying to provide a safe place for children to be so that the parents can go to work and take English language classes. They are trying to provide an environment where parents who may be unfamiliar with the idea of out-of-home care are able to leave children and entrust their children to people they don't know, who don't even speak the same language.

Teachers are trying to create setting in which learning can occur across each of the dimensions we've discussed. They also are trying to plant the seeds of skills that children will need to transition on to the next stages on their journey. They're trying to do everything from guiding children towards tying their own shoes to being able to have conversations with grownups! It's an incredible balancing act that we ask these educators to perform.

SI: I fully agree with what Doug just shared there. I have a recollection of an interesting vignette. I'm not sure if it made it into the book, but it was the educator who talked about the family who had come from Eastern Europe. Every morning the parents would get their kids ready for school. And every morning the grandmother would put on her traditional clothing and help the family. Then she would take up her position near the front door, thinking this might be the day to return home. It's an interesting look at culture within this one family. In terms of collectivist versus individualistic, I think we saw just a little bit of that in our research. Yes, some educators told us their Asian families held different expectations, but we need to remember culture and people exist on a continuum. Different cultures have different expectations and different beliefs and practices. We use the term 'clash of cultures' at times, but I think much of what we documented was talented educators' understanding who's in their room and where they've come from, and their experiences, and what home situations those children are going to after school. This goes back to the foundational idea of authentic inclusion in getting to know these people in appreciation and respect.

MS: And I think in one of our chapters, too, I certainly tried to touch on things like we are talking about groups of people. We're talking about societal culture when we break it down. There are subgroups within those cultures. And then, you know, we've got the individual families that have their own particular ways of believing or not believing or following family tradition. So, there's all of that, in families. The individualistic nature of people is expressed in this sort of family way of doing and agreeing to do certain things together even though they're from individualist cultures.

DI: I'm reminded of the story of Dr Bronfenbrenner feeling at an absolute loss to provide expert testimony on the cases of individual children (recounted in Chapter 4). Perhaps that story helps us untangle some of the threads here between understanding children as individuals and as the product of a myriad of forces, including the pathway that they and their families have taken. We mean that literally with the families in this book. How are these children a product of that pathway, nested within a particular place and a particular cultural background?

Maura, I'm reminded of your metaphor, of the coming together, of the fresh and the salt water, and how there's a blending where estuary meets the sea. I think that we are living in a moment where one hundred million people are in forced migration between settings. In that turmoil, we see clashes of ideas around what is acceptable: around gender roles, around the schooling of girls, around appropriate clothing in school such as the hijab, around attitudes towards corporal punishment, around the place of public institutions in family life, and so on. In many ways, this is an exciting moment to be alive!

MS: Indeed. Some of what you were saying made me think of Bourdieu, about the role of the school to expressly reproduce societal norms and this may also apply to the kindergarten movement. Maybe in America, maybe not so much in Europe, because the kindergarten notion is from Pestalozzi and particularly Froebel, hence the German language about education for very young children, but to have it used for political means is where Bordeaux and others pick it up. In some ways what these children are doing or coming through our schools is actually creating, with all of these preschool considerations, adaptations for literal inclusion of basic facts of other cultures such as Ramadan and Eid, and others like the Diwali festival and so forth are actually challenging these Western philosophical notions of what school is for and how it reproduces traditional society because it's actually serving to do something else, and not reproduce so much as represent a changing society. And so, I think that our educators are doing incredibly deep and philosophical work in their everyday work to be part of humanity and to do their best for their children. Actually what they're doing is a much bigger picture. Talking about integrating, what do you think of the ways in which we are talking about including people in second homelands, especially around the use of assimilation, which seems to be perpetuated in many government policies and grant applications, and very much in the public consciousness to a degree. Do you feel that we have got the potential in early childhood practices, and that which we have had from our participants, that we have the potential to promote the notion of authentic inclusion, and therefore integration, given the very public, and if you like, official perception of assimilation?

SI: I think assimilation is a term that has less use in public schooling. There's a growing consciousness that assimilation is not our goal. I recognise assimilation finds its way into bureaucratic documents and government policies, but I think there's a trend away from it. Also, because we had the advantage of talking to people in five countries, we were able to see that again is on a continuum. It's a term that would not rear its head in New Zealand. But education is really the answer for all these conversations we're having.

MS: May I just stop and challenge you on that? It's the type of education that is given so I would say, education has the potential and what I see in our participants' responses is that they are the people, we want in education. They don't get to make the policies, the vast majority of them just work, have to work with the policies. It's the potential of education rather than current educational practice, that may be the answer to all these things challenging your perception.

DI: You two actually may not be very far apart. Scott, I wonder if you could unpack what you just said? Do you think that the project of education holds the promise of democratising societies? Is it a way to expand opportunity in a sense, or were you saying something different from that?

SI: I think we're on a positive trajectory in terms of where we're going societally. In the five different countries we looked at, while they're each in very different places, they're all on a positive trend. I would say again, the people who are working in the settings, the childcare providers, the playgroups, the day cares, I think in many ways they're ahead of the curve. There are good people in those places who are building society from the ground up and that's powerful. It takes time for people who write the policies to catch up with the people who are doing the work.

DI: Coming at it from a different angle: perhaps John Dewey is right and there is a democratic promise in the project of education, we are democratising the information and skills needed to participate meaningfully in society. Education, beginning in early childhood, can democratise access to the capacity to control the trajectory of one's own life, in many ways.

The other place I might come at the question is around the idea of moving towards a place where inclusion becomes the norm. I think that is very much a political question that is subject to waves of public sentiment and national contexts. We see shifts in the reception of refugees with different governing administrations, for example. In 2017, 43% of refugees resettled to the United States were from predominantly Muslim countries, but in the first year of the

Trump administration, that number fell to 3%, reflecting political agendas, xenophobia, and a desire to protect borders in the wake of 9/11. It's a question about tensions, but I don't see those tensions abating in the short term.

MS: No, I agree. But I think the more widely the notion of inclusion and integration is interpreted and understood, the more the education, maybe, can have an opportunity to perform, as Dewey envisioned in terms of the democratic process. and not so much in the sense of bourgeois reproduction of society. All we can say now is 'Don't shut the door' on opportunities for inclusion, greater understanding of difference, and acceptance of different ways of knowing and doing within the law. These have worked in diverse societies for thousands of years. Let's blend the old wisdoms with the new to create a positive future for these children.

Conclusion

This chapter presented the opportunities for the authors to reflect on the narratives shared by the research participants and to explore their own thinking on the work, creativity, and dedication that is required by all educators, but most particularly those involved in the early years of out-of-home care and with formal education. While the complexity of this work is apparent, even in the relatively homogeneous cohorts that are found in small, traditional communities, it can be overwhelmingly multifaceted in the caring and educational contexts which are multinational, multicultural, and complexly traumatised. There are 'no one size fits all' answers to how best support young children and their families to regain a sense of belonging and to be authentically included as members of new communities and countries. What is clear, however, is that sensitivity, empathy, respect, and creativity, accompanied with genuine acceptance of difference and diversity, are basic steps to facilitating the security, sense of safety, and feelings of belonging that are crucial to these processes for both child and family. As one respondent noted, 'Don't close the door.'

Further Reading

Adelman, C. (2000) Over two years, what did Froebel say to Pestalozzi? *History of Education, 29*(2), 103–114.

Bourdieu, P. (1967). Systems of education and systems of thought. *International Social Science Journal,* 19(3), 367–388.

Bronfenbrenner, U. (1979). *The ecology of human development: Experiments by nature and design.* Harvard University Press.

Dewey, J. (1916). *Democracy and education: An introduction to the philosophy of education.* The Free Press.

Foucault, M. (1977). Panopticism (A. Sheridan, trans.). *Discipline and punish: The birth of the prison* (pp. 195–228). Vintage Books.

Hall, E. (1976). *Beyond culture*. Knopf Doubleday Publishing Group.

Hofstede, G. (2001). *Culture's consequences: Comparing values, behaviors, institutions and organizations across nations* (2nd ed.). Sage.

Hofstede, G., Hofstede, G. J., & Minkov, M. (2010). *Cultures and organisations: Software of the mind*. McGraw-Hill.

Maslow, A. (1943). A theory of human motivation. *Psychological Review*, *50*(4), 370–396.

Pestalozzi, J.H. (1894). *How Gertrude teaches her children* (L.E. Holland & F.C. Turner trans.). Bardeen.

Piaget, J. (1945). *Play, dreams and imitation in childhood*. Heinemann.

Sellars, M., & Imig, D. (2020). Pestalozzi and pedagogies of love: Pathways to educational reform. *Early Child Development and Care*, *191*, 1152–1163. https://doi.org/10.1080/03004430.2020.1845667

Vinje, H. F., Langeland, E., & Bull, T. (2017). Aaron Antonovsky's development of salutogenesis, 1979 to 1994. In M. B. Mittelmark et al. (Eds.), *The Handbook of salutogenesis* (pp. 25–40). Springer International Publishing. https://doi.org/10.1007/978-3-319-04600-6_4

Index

For Product Safety Concerns and Information please contact our EU representative GPSR@taylorandfrancis.com Taylor & Francis Verlag GmbH, Kaufingerstraße 24, 80331 München, Germany

Printed and bound by CPI Group (UK) Ltd, Croydon, CR0 4YY
08/06/2025
01897002-0017